Art Therapy for Groups

ART THERAPY FOR GROUPS

A HANDBOOK OF THEMES, GAMES AND EXERCISES

MARIAN LIEBMANN

ROUTLEDGE

First published 1986 by
Croom Helm Ltd and Brookline Books
Reprinted 1987

Reprinted 1989 and 1991 by Routledge
11 New Fetter Lane
London EC4P 4EE

© 1986 Marian Liebmann

Typeset in Times Roman by
Leaper & Gard Ltd, Bristol, England
Printed and bound in Great Britain by
Billings & Sons Ltd, Worcester

British Library Cataloguing in Publication Data

Liebmann, Marian
   Art therapy for groups: a handbook of themes,
   games and exercises.
   1. Art therapy
   I. Title
   615.8′5156 RC489-A7

   ISBN 0-415-04327-1

Library of Congress Cataloging in Publication Data

Liebmann, Marian, 1942–
   Art therapy for groups
   Bibliography: p.
   Includes index.
   I. Art therapy.   2. Group psychotherapy.
I. Title.
RC489.A7L54   1986   616.89′1656   85-46062

ISBN 0-415-04327-1

Contents

Part Two: Themes, Games and Exercises

Line drawings are by the author.

Photographs

All photographs are printed by David Newton. In the list below, photographers' names appear in brackets. The photographs are not all to the same scale.

Acknowledgements

This book has drawn on the experiences of many people.

First, I would like to thank my tutor, Michael Edwards, who helped me ask the right questions for my dissertation, which was the forerunner of this book. Next, my thanks go to all the art therapists and others who trusted me with their ideas; their names are listed at the back of the book.

Members of Bristol Art Therapy Group have been a great support to me, in encouraging me to produce the original collection, in talking to me about their work and in constructively criticising the manuscript of the present version of the book. Special thanks to Sheena Anderson, Heather Buddery, Paul Curtis, Michael Donnelly, Karen Lee Drucker, John Ford, Linnea Lowes and Roy Thornton.

The participants of the 'Friday Group' (Bristol Art and Psychology Group) took a great interest in the progress of the book in its formative stages. Patricia Brownen and Beryl Tyzack read the whole manuscript, and others commented on small sections.

Experts from other fields helped with booklists: Allan Brown on groupwork, Sue Jennings on dramatherapy, Alison Levinge on music therapy. Sue Jennings also advised on the manuscript, as did my friend June Tillman who is also a writer.

Finally, my thanks to my husband, Mike Coldham, who helped by checking the readability and coherence of the text, as well as providing much practical support; and to my daughter, Anna, for her considerable patience.

Marian Liebmann

Preface

The starting point of this book was my own experience as a member of several groups and the leader of others. I had always been interested in art, and became more and more interested in its potential for the communication of personal matters. I became a staff member at an experimental day centre for adult ex-offenders, and ran sessions there, and also ran day events for church groups and the local encounter centre. At the same time I attended any group art sessions within reach to gain more personal experience. I began to compile a list of games, structures, themes — call them what you will — that other group leaders used, and added them to ones that I or my groups invented. I also became very curious about groups and the structures they used, and how these influenced what went on in the groups.

I decided to pursue this interest further, and in 1979 I enrolled for the MA course in art therapy at Birmingham Polytechnic. For my dissertation I chose to explore my interest in structured art therapy groups, and devised a questionnaire to use as a basis to interview 40 art therapists working in different settings (not all of them were officially called 'art therapists', but they were all using art as a means of personal communication). It was a fascinating learning experience for me, and some of my findings are included in Chapter 1.

One of the purposes I had in mind was to produce a collection of all the themes being used by art therapists, teachers and group leaders. This had to be done after the dissertation, as there was simply too much material to include. With the help of other art therapists in Bristol, the collection was produced in 1982 as a handbook to circulate to those who took part in my survey, and other interested art therapists.

This handbook assumed its readers would all be art therapists experienced in running groups, so it contained no material on this aspect. However, since its publication, there has been widespread interest shown by occupational therapists, social workers, teachers, child guidance workers, community group leaders, peace activists and others. This burgeoning interest shows a need for a new version with more material on how to run groups, and ways in which themes may be used with different groups. These topics form the first half of the book, and the updated collection of themes the second half.

Introduction

Who This Book is For

This book is aimed at professionals in a wide variety of caring professions. They may be art therapists, teachers, social workers, youth workers or community group leaders. Knowledge and experience of working with groups is assumed, so that this book concentrates on how to use art with groups.

However, if you do not have much experience in running groups, there is a list of books on groupwork in the Bibliography. But there is no substitute for experience, and the best way to gain this is to join a variety of groups as a client. This gives you an opportunity both to experience what it feels like to be in the client role and to observe different styles of group leadership.

Before leading your own group it is a good idea to act as co-leader with a more experienced leader or therapist. This gives you a chance to learn from someone more experienced, and also to try out your ideas and skills, and discuss the results.

The same goes for experience of using art with groups. It can be a powerful experience, so it is essential to know what it feels like. Sometimes it is difficult to get started or to make something as you envisaged it, and if you have not experienced this yourself you will not be able to help others when they are stuck.

If there are no suitable personal art or art therapy groups available in your area, write to the British Association of Art Therapists (address at the back of this book), who can put you in touch with their regional representative for advice.

A helpful guideline is always to try out on yourself and your colleagues what you are intending to use with clients. This experience may give you pointers about possible difficulties, iron out organisational wrinkles and demonstrate benefits which can be gained.

The 'Art Therapy' Approach

Art Therapy uses art as a means of personal expression to communicate feelings, rather than aiming at aesthetically pleasing end-products to be judged by external standards. This means of expression is available to everyone, not just the artistically gifted. This rather terse statement is not meant to convey the whole story of art therapy (see Bibliography for art therapy books), but to set the scene for the kind of personal subjective activity this book is about.

It has acquired the name 'Art Therapy' mainly because it has developed most widely in the field of mental health, and especially in hospitals for the mentally ill. This development has been of great benefit to mental patients, but has had the unfortunate side-effect that other groups of people ignore this activity because they do not consider themselves or their clients 'ill'.

However, as will be seen from the examples given further on in Chapter 5, this way of using art can be relevant to many people, whether they are grappling with serious problems or just wish to explore themselves and their feelings, using art as the medium.

In the words of one art therapist, running a group for the general public, 'No special ability or disability is required'.

Art Therapy and Other Fields

Although art therapists have forged the way, there are now many professionals (as mentioned above) who are interested in using art in a personal way with their groups. There is sometimes a problem of language in that different disciplines develop different ways of talking about people and their problems. For instance, the medical world talks of 'illness' and 'therapy', while the social work world may talk of 'social problems' and 'support', and the educational world of 'ignorance' and 'education'. Professionals in these different fields may engage in the same activity — like a personal art group — and call it by different names, such as 'art therapy' or 'social skills' or 'emotional education'. The groups of people may also have different labels — patients, clients or students. The person running the group may be called a therapist, facilitator, leader, teacher, social worker, group worker, etc.

All these different settings suggest different ways of seeing people, and different purposes, which will influence the nature of the activities taking place. But they may all wish to engage in this kind of group art activity.

Because of my background, I shall mostly refer to the person running a group as the 'leader' or '(art) therapist' (since many of my examples are drawn from art therapy), and I shall call the participants of the group 'members' or 'people' (except for examples involving hospital patients or day centre clients). The subject-matter, of course, spans all the other fields implicitly.

Groups and Individuals

Although this collection was made with groups in mind, it can be used by individuals, except for those exercises which require pairs or groups. It is important to make some arrangement for individuals to share their work with someone and to discuss any feelings arising from it.

Ways of Using This Book

If you are new to this kind of work, it will pay dividends to read the whole of the first half. Then, assuming you have some experience of groups, think about the group you are working with, and think about members' individual needs. Pick a relevant exercise and try it out on yourself and your colleagues. After that, introduce it (perhaps with modifications) to your group. The results of that will determine what follows (and see Chapter 2 for more details of how to choose themes).

If you are already familiar with running this kind of group, a good way of using this book is to 'browse' through it, and let it trigger off your own thoughts; you can then choose an exercise and modify it to suit your particular situation, or make up your own entirely.

Limitations of This Book

Some of these have been mentioned already, but they are worth emphasising:

1. This book does not make novices into instant therapists or leaders. Experience, both as a client and as co-leader, is most important.
2. Experience of what is involved in painting or making something is also very important.
3. Not all themes are for everyone. Never use an exercise or theme you feel unhappy with yourself.
4. This book covers groups which meet to share a common activity or theme, and does not cover groups where everyone chooses a different activity.
5. A personal art group will not change peoples' lives — many factors are involved.
6. This book has no guidance about long-term therapeutic work. If you

intend to work in this area, make sure you have the necessary support, supervision and expertise.

7.   There is very little information in this book about the characteristics of different client groups.

8.   This book is an attempt to provide an ordered framework around what is essentially an intuitive process. To use a metaphor, a book on sailing can outline the equipment needed before you start, provide a chart of where dangerous currents might be and give a few accounts of actual sailing trips. It is then up to you to set sail and see what sailing is really like.

PART ONE

ART THERAPY GROUPS

1   *Groupwork, Art Therapy and Games*

This chapter gives some theoretical background to personal art and art therapy groups. It contains some of the findings from my survey of 40 art therapists and group leaders running art groups in a variety of settings. It also gives some of the reasons for using groups and a structured way of working, together with any disadvantages. Finally, it gives a few comments on the place of play and games in art groups.

Why Use Groupwork?

For some leaders and therapists there is a choice between individual work and group work, so it is worth looking at the general reasons for using groupwork. Others, such as teachers, almost always work with groups, and for them the important thing is to maximise the advantages groupwork can have.

The reasons for using groupwork can be summarised as follows:

1. Much of social learning is done in groups; therefore groupwork provides a relevant context in which to practise.
2. People with similar needs can provide mutual support for each other, and help with mutual problem-solving.
3. Group members can learn from the feedback from other members: 'It takes two to see one.'[1]
4. Group members can try new roles, from seeing how others react (role-modelling), and can be supported and reinforced in this.
5. Groups can be catalysts for developing latent resources and abilities.
6. Groups are more suitable for certain individuals, e.g. those who find the intimacy of individual work too intense.
7. Groups can be more democratic, sharing the power and responsibility.
8. Some therapists/group workers find groupwork more satisfying than individual work.

9.   Groups can be an economical way of using expertise to help several people at the same time.

However, there are also some disadvantages:

1.   Confidentiality is more difficult because more people are involved.
2.   Groups need resources and can be difficult to organise.
3.   Less individual attention is available to members of a group.
4.   A group may be 'labelled' or acquire a stigma.[2]

Many of these points are relevant to groups working with art, and were borne out in my survey. For this survey, I interviewed art therapists working in a wide variety of treatment and educational settings: general psychiatric and day hospitals, probation and social services day centres, schools, adolescent units, art therapy colleges, adult education institutes. They were working with an even wider cross-section of the community: long-stay and geriatric patients, acute psychiatric patients, mentally handicapped, ex-offenders, social work clients, alcoholics, families, children, art therapists and social workers in training.[3]

I asked all the therapists what purposes their groups had, and the answers seemed to fall into two clusters: personal and social. These are summarised in Tables 1 and 2.[4]

Table 1: General Personal Purposes (not in any order)

---

1. Creativity and spontaneity
2. Confidence-building, self-validation, realisation of own potential
3. Increase personal autonomy and motivation, develop as individual
4. Freedom to make decisions, experiment, test out ideas
5. Express feelings, emotions, conflicts
6. Work with fantasy and unconscious
7. Insight, self-awareness, reflection
8. Ordering of experience visually and verbally
9. Relaxation

Table 2: General Social Purposes (not in any order)

---

1. Awareness, recognition, and appreciation of others
2. Co-operation, involvement in group activity
3. Communication
4. Sharing of problems, experiences and insights
5. Discovery of universality of experience/uniqueness of individual
6. Relate to others in a group, understanding of effect of self on others, and relationships
7. Social support and trust
8. Cohesion of group
9. Examine group issues

As the tables show, art therapists saw their groups as aiming to enhance and sometimes change the personal and social functioning of the group members, rather than as a specific treatment for a particular disease. Their aims also tie in with Yalom's curative factors for group therapy:

1. Instillation of hope
2. Universality
3. Imparting of information
4. Altruism
5. The corrective recapitulation of the primary family group
6. Development of socialising techniques
7. Imitative behaviour
8. Interpersonal learning
9. Group cohesiveness
10. Catharsis
11. Existential factors (such as inevitability of death)[5]

This enhancement of personal and social functioning is obviously applicable in a wide variety of settings, whether social, educational or therapeutic, and can include almost anyone who can function independently. Nor do these aims have to be confined to those labelled as in need of special help; they are human qualities we are all striving for, at one time or another. In fact, many of the art therapists interviewed run workshops of a similar kind for people in the wider community, who want to explore themselves and enhance their personal skills and feelings.

Why Use Art?

So far most of the reasons and purposes given apply to any kind of group. It is worth drawing out the aspects of groupwork which are particularly enhanced by using art as the group activity:

1. Everyone can join in at the same time, at their own level. The process of the activity is important, and a scribble can be as much of a contribution as a finished painting.
2. Art can be another important avenue of communication and expression, especially when words fail. The spatial character of pictures can describe many aspects of experience simultaneously.
3. Art facilitates creativity.
4. Art is useful in working with fantasy and unconscious.
5. Art products are tangible and can be examined at a later time.
6. Art can be enjoyable, and in a group this can lead to shared pleasure.[6]

To summarise, art therapy or personal art groups can provide a combination of individual and group experiences which draw on the traditions of both groupwork and art therapy.

What Size of Group is Best?

Most art therapy and personal art groups, in common with other 'small groups', have a membership of between six and twelve, although larger groups are occasionally manageable. This size is important to ensure the following factors:

1. Members can maintain visual and verbal contact with all other members.
2. Group cohesiveness can be achieved.
3. There is an opportunity for each person to have an adequate share of time in discussion.
4. There are enough people to encourage interaction and a free flow of ideas, and to undertake group projects.[7]

What is a Structured Art Group?

Some art therapy groups work in a 'non-structured' way; that is, the group meets as a group at a specific time and place, but apart from that everyone pursues his or her own work. There is absolutely nothing wrong with this, and it is a good way of working for groups of people who all know what they want to do. However, the purpose of this book is to look at 'structured' art therapy groups; that is, those which meet to share a common task or explore a common theme.

Of course, many groups will combine elements of both, and alternate between structured work and sessions in which everyone 'does their own thing'. Figure 1 shows the continuum of possibilities.[8]

Figure 1: Continuum of Possibilities for Work in Art Therapy Groups

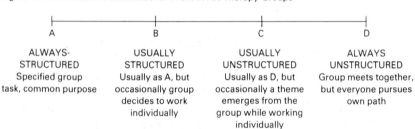

A	B	C	D
ALWAYS-STRUCTURED	USUALLY STRUCTURED	USUALLY UNSTRUCTURED	ALWAYS UNSTRUCTURED
Specified group task, common purpose	Usually as A, but occasionally group decides to work individually	Usually as D, but occasionally a theme emerges from the group while working individually	Group meets together, but everyone pursues own path

Working in a 'structured' way can mean many things. It can mean using just a simple boundary rule, such as 'Paint what you like, but use only three colours.' Or it can mean a more prescribed activity, such as 'Choose one crayon and have a non-verbal conversation with another person on the same piece of paper.' Again, there is a continuum from instructions which are so loose that they do not constitute a theme at all, to activities which could be described as very specific themes.[9]

This can be illustrated by looking at some different possible introductions:

1. We are going to 'do our own thing'.
2. Use a large sheet of paper and your three favourite colours to draw a picture of anything you like.
3. Start with a doodle and see if it turns into anything.
4. Paint a childhood incident.
5. Paint a childhood incident which was a turning point.
6. Paint your first experience of separation.
7. Paint your first day at school.

The first one is obviously not a theme, although even to say 'Do your own thing' is a certain kind of structure. The second and third are structured ways of starting, but do not specify anything further. The last four are recognisably 'themes', and progressively more specific. It is sometimes worth being fairly specific, if the aim is to share common experiences, but not so specific that there is no room for individual choice and interpretation of the theme, at whatever level is appropriate. So, for a group of adults, the last one on the list might be too specific as it does not leave room for anyone who cannot or does not want to remember their first day at school.

Why Use Structured Art Groups?

Some of the reasons for using themes, structures, exercises, techniques and games with art groups are given below. It is worth reflecting on them to see if they apply to your group.

1. Many people have great difficulty in starting. A theme can give a focus to begin somewhere.
2. Some initial themes can help groups understand what art therapy is all about. This is especially true if people in the group are not familiar with the approach, and see the art group only in terms of former school art lessons or external aesthetic standards.

3. Some groups are very insecure and need structure if they are to operate at all.
4. There is often pressure of time. For community groups and training courses, the art group may be only one session, or a day, or a weekend. Even in hospitals and day centres, many people only stay a short time, in order to return to normal life as quickly as possible. A group can get to the point more quickly if it focuses on a suitable theme.
5. Sharing a theme can help to weld a group together.
6. Themes and exercises can be interpreted on many levels and used flexibly to meet different needs. The group can be involved in the choice of theme if this is appropriate.
7. Certain themes can be useful in helping members of the group to relate to each other.
8. Sometimes themes can help people to get out of 'ruts' by facilitating work and discussion which would otherwise not happen.[10]

Using themes to the best advantage presupposes all the experience and preparation mentioned in the Introduction. If used inappropriately, some themes can evoke feelings which are too much for that group to handle at that time. At the other end of the spectrum, some can lead to a superficial experience which leaves people dissatisfied. Between these two poles there is a wide variety of group experiences using art structures which can be interesting and revealing, and also enjoyable.

Art and Play

There is now a vast literature on play, and it is impossible to do justice to it in a few paragraphs. These comments are meant to stimulate thought and ideas, which can be followed up by consulting the titles on play in the Bibliography.

Piaget has classified play into three types:

1. Sensori-motor play, in which a child seeks to master a skill, and then repeats it for the sheer enjoyment (ages 0-2 yrs).
2. Symbolic play, in which a child plays 'pretend' games using objects to hand as symbols for other things, e.g. she/he may pick up a stone and pretend it is an ice-cream, saying 'Here is an ice-cream for you. Eat it!' (ages 2-6 yrs).
3. Games with rules, in which a change of rules changes the nature of the game. These may often involve groups (age 6+).[11]

Although the classification above refers to stages of development, all three types of play may be involved in the use of art. The first type will be part of exploring the use of art materials, and the activities concerned with 'media exploration' (see Section C in Part Two) will encourage this kind of play, for both children and adults (who often wish they could recapture children's play capacity). The second type is part of the nature of art, which is a symbolic medium; any painted image stands for something in the artist's mind. The third type of play can be involved in some of the art communication group games, which are described more fully in the next section of this chapter. Many artists have used these elements of play to explore and experiment with media to produce new forms and unexpected results.

However, this classification of types of play only goes so far. Play can never be defined as one particular activity; rather, it comprises many kinds of activity, linked by an attitude of non-literalness and enjoyment, known as 'playfulness'. For instance, the same activity may be playful or non-playful: two people chasing each other may be involved in a serious situation, but if at the same time they are laughing it is usually safe to assume they are playing. The characteristics of play may be summarised as follows:

1. Play is pleasurable and enjoyable.
2. Play has no extrinsic goals; it is inherently unproductive.
3. Play is spontaneous and voluntary, and freely chosen.
4. Play involves active engagement on the part of the player.
5. Play is related to what is not play.[12]

Thus, play is a free, joyful activity — but also needs the limits outlined above in order to be play. It is also usually a social activity.

The fifth quality on the list of characteristics is one which engages many teachers and therapists. It is well known that children's play is linked to their learning of language and other cognitive skills, and to their practising of social roles. At another level, children also re-enact problems and conflicts in a condensed form in their play. The non-literal quality of play means that this can be done in safety, without fear of real consequences. By representing a difficult experience symbolically, and going through it again, perhaps changing the outcome, a child becomes more able to deal with the problem in real life.[13]

Adults too need to develop or rediscover a sense of play, which can give them a much-needed 'space' away from the constraints of normal living, and help them to renew their capacities for tackling life's problems and opportunities. In Winnicott's words: '*It is play that is the universal,* and that belongs to health: playing facilitates growth and therefore health; playing leads into group relations; playing can be a form of communication in psychotherapy ...'[14]

Art Games

Games can be seen as play activities which have become institutionalised. They belong to Piaget's third stage of play, involving explicit rules, which make up the very essence of the game. Games are social activities, and the participants need to agree on the rules before they can take part in the game. However, there need be nothing sacrosanct about the rules — they can be changed at will to produce an entirely new game. In a worthwhile game the rules will be flexible enough to allow for many levels of response, resulting in an enjoyable playful activity.[15]

Many group leaders have found that games can stimulate enjoyable learning experiences, and there has been a burgeoning of literature on 'growth games', 'new games', 'co-operative games' — to mention just a few. Leaders in informal settings often use games to start sessions, or to help people to make contact with each other.

Of course, a 'games' approach does not suit everyone: some people feel it would take away from the seriousness of their work, and the respect of other professionals for them. This depends to some extent on the ethos of the setting in which the activities take place.[16]

However, many group art activities can be seen as games, in the sense that they are based on certain simple rules contained within the theme, which is usually flexible enough to allow for many levels of response.[17] Then, starting with a particular theme, we could change the rules and see how this changes the activity. It is easier to see how this might work if we look at a practical example.

For instance, the theme 'Draw an advertisement for yourself' can be interpreted on several different levels. It could be an opportunity to display or acknowledge one's best points (which modesty and our self-deprecating culture often do not allow); or to discover some new assets in the process of doing the picture; or to learn about others; or to select qualities which appeal to certain kinds of other people (as advertisements are aimed at particular targets); or to consider whether we are different with different kinds of people.

Then we could also change the rules slightly by adding that, when each person has drawn their own self-advertisement, others in the group add qualities that have been missed; or the group members can select from others' 'wares' or 'trade' them; there are many possibilities. All these changes will produce an effect which will make it a different activity or game.[18] Most of the changes suggested above make the activity more of an interactive group game, which can only take place properly if everyone joins in. Many personal themes can be turned into group games in this way, and Section J in Part Two contains some of these. Compare, for instance, how theme 89 (Metaphorical Portraits) can be changed into a group game (204).

One of the most valuable qualities of play and games is the provision of a parallel frame of reference to 'real life', in which different 'ways of being' can be tried out without any 'real life' consequences. Small risks can be attempted before large ones. Perhaps someone doing the 'advertisement' exercise might be helped to acknowledge some good qualities. The next step, in the day-to-day world, might be to let others know about these good qualities, instead of hiding them.

Games can also provide indirect approaches to matters of moment which may be difficult or painful to confront directly. They can give rise to a lot of fun and hilarity, but also at the same time be quite serious. Three art therapists who see some of their structured art activities as games commented:

Therapist A: 'A game is a collection of loosely bound rules with a light-hearted feel, which can lead unwittingly into pertinent areas — though it needn't do that.'

Therapist B: 'Games relax people, give them confidence and enjoyment, and can also be revealing.'

Therapist C: 'Games are more than formal structures, because they are playful and a source of pleasure.'[19]

In this sense it is possible to regard many art group themes as art games, with a set of rules adopted for that game, and a non-literal frame of reference. An example of this might be the use made of the Metaphorical Portraits game at a day workshop (see Chapter 5, Example 14), where one woman drew another as a brick wall with a green tree peeping out behind (see Photograph 13). Here the game structure provided a framework which made it possible for them to refer, in a non-literal way, to their difficult relationship in a way they had not been able to before. The presence of the tree signified hope and change, and the two women were able to discuss this, leading to a fresh start in communicating with each other.

Another way in which leaders and therapists use games is to 'warm up' before a main activity or theme. The main aim here is to get people moving and to help them feel at ease in the group; and to encourage spontaneity.

Some themes lend themselves to being seen as art games more than others. The important elements are the use of a structured activity, in which rules are flexible and can be changed; and above all, an attitude of playfulness and enjoyment, which does not detract from the possible seriousness of the theme.

Conclusion

This chapter has given some theoretical framework to the reasons for using groupwork and for using art in groupwork. It has looked at the contribution that themes and structures can make. Finally, it has looked at the role of play in art activities, and at the way art games can be developed. All this forms a useful background in thinking about groups, before embarking on the practical steps of running a group, which is the topic of the next chapter.

References

1. S.A. Culbert, 'The Interpersonal Process of Self-Disclosure: It Takes Two to See One', *Explorations in Applied Behavioral Science*, No. 3 (Renaissance Editions, New York, 1967).

2. A. Brown, *Groupwork* (Heinemann, London, 1979), pp. 11-12.

3. M.F. Liebmann, 'A Study of Structured Art Therapy Groups', unpublished MA thesis, Birmingham Polytechnic, 1979.

4. Ibid., p. 27.

5. I.D. Yalom, *The Theory and Practice of Group Psychotherapy* (Basic Books, New York, 1975), p. 71.

6. M.F. Liebmann, 'Art Games and Group Structures' in T. Dalley (ed.), *Art as Therapy* (Tavistock, London, 1984), p. 159.

7. T. Douglas, *Groupwork Practice* (Tavistock, London, 1976), pp. 85-6.

8. Liebmann, 'A Study of Structured Art Therapy Groups', p. 28.

9. Ibid., pp. 38-40.

10. Ibid., pp. 41-2.

11. J. Piaget, *Play, Dreams and Imitation in Childhood* (Routledge and Kegan Paul, London, 1951; W.W. Norton, New York, 1962); C. Garvey, *Play* (Fontana/Open Books, London, 1977), pp. 13-14.

12. Garvey, *Play*, p. 10.

13. E.Erikson, *Toys and Reasons* (Marion Boyars, London, 1978), pp. 29-39.

14. D.W. Winnicott, *Playing and Reality* (Pelican, Harmondsworth, 1974), p. 48.

15. J. Huizinga, *Homo Ludens* (Temple-Smith, London, 1970), p. 47.

16. Liebmann, 'A Study of Structured Art Therapy Groups', pp. 68-71.

17. Ibid., pp. 70-1.

18. Ibid., pp. 127-8.

19. Ibid., p. 70.

2   *Running a Group*

Before starting on some of the practicalities of running a group, it is worth remembering that the whole purpose of the group is to provide a warm, trusting environment in which people can feel at ease in revealing personal matters. Caring and respect for other people, and for their feelings and points of view, are a priority. The suggestions given in this chapter are designed to help to achieve this kind of caring client-centred group which people enjoy being in.

There are several points to think about in relation to running a group, and a checklist of them is useful:

1. Setting up the group
2. Outside factors affecting the group
3. Aims and goals
4. Group boundaries and ground rules
5. Open and closed groups
6. Leadership roles
7. Usual pattern for session
8. Introductions and 'warming up'
9. Choosing an activity or theme
10. The activity
11. Discussion
12. Interpretation
13. Ending the session
14. Recording and evaluation
15. Alternative patterns of sessions
16. Group process over time

The rest of the chapter will look briefly at each of these aspects in turn. For further information on groupwork, please see the Bibliography.

1. Setting Up the Group

This is often the hardest part, and requires a good deal of time and energy to achieve. These are the points that need to be worked out and settled:

Leader(s)

Are there suitable and experienced leaders for this workshop, or this on-going group?
Does there need to be a co-leader?
Is payment involved?
What is the insurance provision?

Room

Is there a suitable room, and is it large enough?
Where is the key kept?
Is the room light enough in daylight or artificial light?
Is there access to a sink and water?
Are there tables and chairs?
Is there enough floor space for what you want to do?
Is there room for paintings to dry?
Where will you hold discussions of work done?
Will the room dictate using dry media only?
Will the room be quiet enough?
Do you need facilities to make drinks, or serve food?
Where is the First Aid box, and is it complete?

Time

Is there a suitable slot on the institutional timetable?
What activities will come before and after, which might influence the art session?
If it is a single session, such as an evening or day workshop, which day and what time are best?

Materials

Which of the materials listed below do you want to include?

Paints — powder or liquid (the latter are more expensive, but are easier to use and need no preparation).
Utensils for handling paint, e.g. spoons for powder paint.
Palettes for holding paints and mixing them (yoghurt trays from super-markets can be useful as disposable palettes).
Water jars.
Brushes — large and small.

Dry media — wax crayons, felt-tip pens, oil pastels, conté crayons, charcoal.

Paper — sugar paper, lining paper, cartridge paper, newsprint rolls; different colours and sizes.

Card — thin or thick — for three-dimensional work.

Clay and boards (and some means of keeping clay damp and cool; also some means of cutting individual lumps off, such as cheese-wire).

Collage materials — magazines, textured materials, fabrics, etc.

Scissors, knife.

Adhesives — glue for collage and three-dimensional work; sellotape.

Rags and paper tissues for wiping up.

Newspaper or polythene sheet to cover up tables or carpet, or for paintings to dry on.

Many of these will need buying or ordering well in advance, especially if you work in an institution which orders all its equipment from certain suppliers.

Members of Group

This is probably the most tricky of all. You may need a referral system, which you will need to explain to other staff. How can they easily know who is going to benefit from the art group you are going to run? You may need to talk to other staff about the sort of 'ready-made' groups (e.g. a ward, a class, an old people's home) which would gain from regular art therapy or personal art sessions. One good way of introducing this activity is to have a workshop for other staff first, so that they have a first-hand knowledge of what is involved, and also have a chance to ask questions about any misgivings they may have. If you are working in an institution, it is important to get as much support as possible for what you are doing before you start.

If you are running a workshop for members of the community (e.g. a day workshop for people working in the caring professions), you will need to think about posters and how to word them to attract those you want (and perhaps deflect those you do not feel you can cope with). You will need to leave plenty of time for publicity, and also to think about costs and payment.

2. Outside Factors Affecting the Group

These are the factors over which you may have no control, but which may affect your group. Many of them have been mentioned in the previous section.

Institutional Factors

Your group will be bound by institutional timetables, such as mealtimes, times of transport, shift changes, break-times, etc. It will also be affected by the amount of support there is for you and your kind of work, e.g. if there is little support you may be subject to interruptions, or find group members suddenly withdrawn. If there is good support there will be respect for you and what your group needs, perhaps other staff helping, and interest shown in the results. Sometimes there can be problems if the aims of the group are different from the aims of the institution, or if group members receive different messages from different therapists or staff members.

Physical Factors

An art group can be affected very much by the space at its disposal. Groups which have to take place in small, dark, claustrophobic rooms are restricted in what they can achieve — as are groups in rooms which are 'through-routes' to other rooms and subject to constant interruptions. Noise from adjacent rooms, lack of suitable tables and presence of unsuitable carpets can further inhibit groups. By contrast, a quiet, light room with a messy painting area and a comfortable discussion space, can do much to enhance a group's experience.

Clientele

This will, of course, be the most important factor determining what you can and cannot expect to do with your group. Obviously, different groups will have different needs and be able to cope with different activities. You may be working with long-term schizophrenic patients in a hospital, ex-offenders in a day centre, children and young people in 'intermediate treatment', a social services staff team, acute admissions patients in a mental hospital, cancer patients in the community, elderly people attending a day centre or a group of mentally handicapped adults, to name but a few client groups. They may bring a wide variety of problems with them, which need to be taken into account. Elderly and handicapped people may need wheelchairs or have difficulty with vision and hearing; steps can sometimes be taken to help with these. Physically ill people may be very tired and in considerable pain, and therefore have limited concentration. Children, mentally handicapped people and some elderly dementing patients also have very short concentration spans. In any of these groups, there may be a lot in common between members, or a great mixture of sometimes incompatible people. There will be different levels of insight and awareness; sometimes there may be inappropriate people present, who can be disruptive.

Feelings

People arrive at a group session bringing with them feelings from all sorts of other situations, whether from the outside world or from elsewhere within an institution. They may be feeling flat, high, anxious, preoccupied or simply very tired. It is a good idea to check how people are feeling at the beginning of a session — it may influence your choice of activity or help you realise your opportunities or likely limitations to achievement that session. If an art session does not go very well, it may not be because of what has happened in the group, but because of something else that happened outside it. In some institutions the art session is part of a planned programme (e.g. in many day centres), and you need to be aware of what has gone before.

3. Aims and Goals

It is important to be clear about (at least some of) your aims and goals. It may help to look at the lists in Tables 1 and 2 in Chapter 1 to see which aims and goals you have in mind for your group. You may have other aims which are important. Ask yourself why this group has come together for an art session. Here are a few examples of different aims:

A group of acute admissions patients is exploring what brought them into hospital.

A group of caring professionals may want to find out what art therapy is all about.

A women's group experiencing a 'sticky patch' is trying the use of art as a non-verbal means of communication.

A group of mentally handicapped adults is exploring their creativity.

A group of elderly people in a day centre is using the art group to reflect on their lives, both happy and unhappy events.

A single session for cancer patients aims to open some doors for them to explore further on their own.

A day workshop for a church group may seek to involve adults and children in activities which both can use equally well for meaningful communication.

(Note: Some of the above groups are described in some detail in Chapter 5.)

4. Group Boundaries and Ground Rules

Every group needs a few 'ground rules' to know where it stands, and for members to know what is expected, and (just as important) not expected.

Some of these will be worked out beforehand, such as whether there is a 'contract' to attend a certain number of sessions, and whether certain people need to be excluded (e.g. because previous experience has shown that they are disruptive and the group cannot operate properly with them in it).

Others will need to be established when the group starts. Many of these will be implicitly assumed by those with group experience, but may need emphasising for those new to groupwork. Some need to be worked out with group members. Here are some to consider:

Normal social rules, e.g. no interrupting, respect for others, arriving on time, etc.

Practical details if appropriate — toilets, breaks, drinks, food, etc.

The importance of confidentiality, so that the group can feel safe.

Participation: it is vital to let people know if they are expected to participate and to talk about their work, and also if this is not required.

Time limits need to be spelled out (and whether people are expected to stay all the time), so that people can avoid being left with 'unfinished business' when the groups ends.

Talking during the activity: is this to be encouraged or discouraged? Many therapists and leaders feel the experience of painting is more intense if there is no talking, but some use painting as a means of enabling talking to start.

Smoking: to be allowed or not?

Decide whether you as leader are going to join in or not (see Section 6).

Group responsibility: decide what this means. It may mean everyone being responsible for their own feelings; or everyone joining in the discussion; or everyone helping to choose the theme. It may also mean everyone helps with the clearing up!

5. Open and Closed Groups

One important decision to be made is whether the group is to be a closed or an open group. A closed group usually runs for a fixed number of sessions with the same members; this means that members can get to know each other well, and build up trust, to share at a deep level. An open group allows people to join and leave as they wish, and consequently remains at a fairly superficial level. Many groups in day hospitals and day centres are closed groups with a commitment to attend. However, groups for in-patients are more likely to be open groups, as patients are discharged as soon as possible to prevent disruption to their lives, and institutionalisation.

Semi-open groups are a useful compromise. There is usually a commitment to attend, but membership changes slowly as people leave and newcomers arrive. In this way the group ethos is maintained, while allowing for a natural or an organised turnover. This kind of group is also usual in many day hospitals and day centres, and also in many ongoing community groups.

6. Leadership Roles

There are many styles of leadership, and observation of other group leaders is most helpful in deciding which style is suitable for you and your group. It is also worth consulting some books on groupwork. A few points are worth emphasising here:

Presence of a Co-leader

This can be very valuable, as it means there are two people to discuss how to run the group in the first place, and this can avoid many pitfalls. In the session itself, a co-leader can provide a 'model' for group members, can support the leader and (if necessary) go and help a group member who leaves suddenly. After the session, two heads are better than one at evaluation. It is most important to work out the roles beforehand, as there is nothing worse than two leaders at cross-purposes!

Joining In

Most leaders and therapists join in the actual painting or other activity session because they feel, that if they expect others to participate and to be open, then they ought to set an example. In this way, they are demonstrating that they are also members of the group, rather than aloof observers. However, there are also some very sound reasons for not joining in, such as concentrating on the organisation of materials for group members, or being available to group members on an individual basis, or concentrating on observation where this is judged the most important task of the leader. This decision has to be an individual one, according to the needs of the group and the personal philosophy of the therapist or leader. If leaders do participate, they need to ensure that they do not become so immersed in their own work that they fail to pay attention to the group, which is, after all, their primary task.

Group Involvement

Some groups look very much to the leader, and this can be quite appropriate. The leader initiates the sessions and most of the comments are directed at him/her. In other groups, the leader consciously tries to involve the group as democratically as possible. Initially this may mean encouraging group members, in discussion time, to ask questions and make comments directly to other group members. As time goes on, members of the group may help to choose themes for the group, and be more involved in the general running, e.g. help new members find their feet, etc. They may also relate more to other members.

Transference and Projections

This is a term which is sometimes used in groups with a psychotherapeutic orientation. It describes the tendency of group members to 'transfer' feelings for significant figures in their lives on to the group leader or therapist. They may, for instance, 'project' their continued need for a parent on to the group leader. This may lead to over-dependence on the leader, or to conflict with him or her, according to previous experience. In institutions, this is often enhanced by the fact that doctors and therapists are seen as having considerable power and authority.

If you are involved in a group which works with these projections, you will probably already be involved in some further training in this connection. An excellent book to consult is *The Theory and Practice of Group Psychotherapy* by I.D. Yalom, but, of course, this is no substitute for experiential training.

However, many groups do not use these terms, nor make specific use of these facts in their way of working. Nevertheless, it is worth being aware of what is happening, even if only to acknowledge it (see example in Chapter 3); or to take appropriate action. For example, an art therapist working with a community group over several months (see Chapter 4), was approached by a group member with a request for individual therapy. She had become aware of his increasing dependence on her, and suspected that he saw her in a parental role and wanted her to be his individual therapist. She acknowledged his need, but felt it would be inappropriate for her to fulfil it, and gave him the name of another therapist who was not involved with the group.

7. Usual Pattern for Session

Most sessions have a similar format:
Introduction and 'warming up': 10-30 minutes
    followed by
Activity: 20-45 minutes
    followed by
Discussion and ending of group: 30-45 minutes.[1]
In many institutions the time available is $1\frac{1}{2}$-2 hours, and the timings given above fit into these. For community groups and professionals, longer times could be more appropriate, with more time allowed for both the activity and the discussion.

There are other formats, which will be discussed later. Each of the stages mentioned above will be described now in more detail, together with some suggestions on how to choose an appropriate activity or theme.

8. Introductions and 'Warming up'

Introductions

The main aim of the initial phase of a group session is to bring people together, help them to 'arrive' and to relax before they plunge into an experience that may be new, difficult or strenuous.

You can do a lot to encourage a good atmosphere just by the welcome you give to the group members, whether they have arrived from afar, or are resident in the institution where the session takes place.

If people have travelled some distance, a good way to start can be by having hot drinks available. This can also help to smooth over the awkward period at the beginning when not everyone has arrived and it is inappropriate to make a start.

If people do not already know each other, it is essential to spend some time on introductions. As well as names, it helps to ask for a small piece of introductory information, e.g. why people have come, what they are hoping to get from the session(s) or a bit of personal information. Sometimes it is a good idea to structure this and ask for, say, people's hobbies, to avoid the stereotyped responses and 'pigeon-holing' (as well as the awkwardness for those without jobs). The aim of this time is for people to get to know each other a little, so that they feel more comfortable working together. It can also help you, as leader, to get a feel for the people in the group and their interest in it, and this can be helpful in running the session.

If a session is one of a series, it may still be necessary to introduce any newcomers, and explain to them what the group is about. It is important to check how people are feeling and what is on their minds, especially if the group takes place in an institution. Expressing some of these thoughts and feelings can sometimes help people to 'arrive' mentally, and can also possibly provide pointers for a theme for the session.

In this introductory session you also need to spell out any ground rules, or get the group to agree on certain points, e.g. smoking, timing, breaks, toilets, participation, talking, etc. (see Section 4 in this chapter). You will also need to explain the nature of the activity, what art therapy is or the personal nature of this art group. Some of the phrases that can be useful are:
... not about producing beautiful works of art;
... painting as we did when we were children — spontaneously;
... exploring in an open-ended way;
... no 'right' way of doing it;
... expressing our feelings using art materials;
... using art in a personal way;
... no special ability or disability;
... complete statements and finished images are not looked for — scribbles and marks are fine;
... relax and use the media in whatever way you want.

Obviously, not all these remarks are suitable for all groups, and you will have to choose and adapt what you say to your group.

Probably a word or two about the materials available will be a good idea, especially if some of the group members have not used them before, or for a long time. The more relaxed people are about using the materials, the more freely and spontaneously they will be able to use them.

'Warm-up' Activities

This can be a physical activity or an introductory painting activity.

Physical 'warm-up' activities include such things as: shoulder rubs, milling round and shaking hands, circle dances, etc., which help to get energy flowing. There is a short list of these in Part Two, Section B of this book. If you are interested in developing their use further, there are several excellent books listed in the Bibliography in Part Two, Section P (subsections 3 and 7).

Painting 'warm-up' activities include such things as: passing a piece of paper around for everyone to make a mark; a quick drawing of what is on people's minds; introducing oneself in a picture. There is a list of suggestions in Part Two, Section B, and many themes can be adapted for use as 'warm ups'. The drawings or paintings done at this stage are usually shared before moving on to the main activity or theme.

In an established group, introductions and 'warm-up' activities may not be needed each time. The group comes together, has a brief discussion about the session's theme, and then everyone gets straight on with the activity. This is possible because the 'ground rules' and way of working have been worked out and have become an implicit part of the group. If new people join, these 'rules' will have to be explained. From time to time, an established group will need to spend some discussion time to reassess its way of working and its ground rules, and possibly to agree on some change if it seems appropriate.

9. Choosing an Activity or Theme

There are rather different considerations for groups which meet regularly and for single-occasion groups.

Groups Meeting Regularly

To start the group, a fairly general theme is needed, to help people to get to know each other and their concerns. Possible starting themes might be:

(a) Getting to know the media, playing with paint, possibly using wet paper, and developing something from it (see Part Two, Section C, No. 19)

(b) Any activity from the Media Exploration section (Part Two, Section C)
(c) Introductions (see Part Two, Section F, No. 80)
(d) Lifelines (see Part Two, Section F, No. 91)
(e) How you are feeling, current preoccupations

These are just a few ideas — the main thing is to get people started and to be sensitive to their needs.

There are several ways of trying to work out how to choose an appropriate theme from one session to the next:

(a) Between sessions, work out what would follow on best and devise an appropriate theme. For example, in a mental hospital acute ward, at the end of one session the discussion was about loneliness. The art therapist worked out a series on friendship (see Part Two, Section F, No. 114).
(b) Where the art session is part of an overall programme, there may be pointers from other sessions. For example, in a day hospital using art therapy, psychodrama, yoga, psychotherapy and discussion, the art therapy session took place the day after the psychodrama session. The staff team met between the sessions to work out suitable themes for the art session, based on what had emerged from the psychodrama session.
(c) Look at the paintings from the previous session (usually the previous week) with the group, to see whether people have any fresh thoughts on them. See what theme emerges from this discussion.
(d) If a particular problem in group relationships seems to be impeding the group's progress, a group painting can often show this up, so that it can be discussed. For example, in a day hospital group, one particular man hid behind his paintings. A group painting showed his contribution squeezed into a corner, demonstrating to the whole group how 'marginalised' he felt.
(e) If a change of direction seems to be required, think through what is needed and select an appropriate theme.

In most of the options so far, the therapist or leader takes a large measure of responsibility for choosing the theme, and this can be appropriate, although it does mean that the choice is very much influenced by the leader's view of members' needs. Where there is a thread of continuity, the group also has a feeling of making progress, step by step, and this can be encouraging. However, the disadvantage of these options is that they are not able to take account of the more immediate feelings and moods of the group. The following options show how these can be included:

(f) The warm-up session or introductory 'round of feelings' can lead to a choice of theme. For example, in one group of young adults there were a lot of feelings about parents, so the leader suggested a theme on family life. Possibilities could be:

'How I see myself fitting into family life'
'What I got from my Mum and my Dad'
'Likes and dislikes about my family'
'The family set-up in diagram form'

(g) The 'round of feelings' could be based on what people felt after the previous week's session, and this could lead to the next theme, as above.

(h) If the leader usually introduces a theme without a 'round of feelings', it can be good to have a choice of themes, so that the group can choose.

(i) In peer groups, such as staff training groups, a list can be passed round for people to choose what they want to explore.

Any theme chosen should be flexible enough for anyone to interpret in their own way, according to their needs.

Some practical points will need to be borne in mind. Group paintings and murals need preparation, rooms have to be rearranged for group projects, special materials have to be organised.

There is no 'right' way of choosing a theme. It is a matter for each leader or therapist to work out in the most appropriate way, according to their own preferred style, the needs of the group and the facilities at their disposal.

Single-occasion Groups

The choice of theme here depends very much on the aims and goals of the group (see Section 3 of this chapter). Here are some examples of themes chosen. (Some of these groups are described more fully in Chapter 5, and all the themes are explained in Part Two of this book):

Residential children's workers attending an in-service training course were asked to start by joining in a group mural. After discussion, this was followed by the theme 'My Family Tree', each person drawing their own family as a tree. This gave rise to discussion of family experiences as seen from a child's point of view.

A women's group experiencing difficulties did a group drawing in which each person had a different coloured crayon and contributed in turn. The resulting patterns of communication were discussed.

A group of cancer patients finding it difficult to contemplate the future did paintings on the theme of journeys they wanted to make.

An introductory day for a church group containing adults and children:

Introductions — name and a personal interest

Round Robin drawings (see Part Two, Section J, No. 211)

Conversation in paint, with one partner
Paint yourself as a kind of food
Lunch (shared)
Group story on long sheet of paper, made up of everyone's individual
    stories, interwoven in silence (see Part Two, Section I, No. 181)
Writing based on group story
Group collage
An introductory evening for a group of professionals:
How I am feeling
Conversation in paint, in pairs
Group painting (no theme)
An afternoon for a peace education group:
Introduce yourself in a picture
Painting in pairs
Group painting on theme of 'What peace means to me'

In all these examples, plenty of time was allowed for discussion after each
activity and at the end.

Themes in Relation to Client Groups

One might think that using a particular theme would always have the same
outcome. This is hardly ever the case! The following example demonstrates
this. Three different art therapists, commenting on the theme 'Draw an
advertisement for yourself', had very different experiences:

Therapist D: 'The purpose of this is to look at positive self-image. It is
useful with a particularly depressed group — lots of positive feedback from group members to other individuals.'
Therapist E: 'A difficult theme which needs careful introduction, but
can become very negative, I've found.'
Therapist F: 'I usually suggest that people consider not only those
aspects of themselves which are worth while, but also
what kind of people they wish to attract ... becoming con-
scious of how one presents oneself publicly is a difficult
enterprise, and people often present their disabilities and
uncertainties rather than their abilities and good points.'[2]

The first two of these were working with in-patients and day patients in a
hospital, and the third was working in a social services day centre for ex-
psychiatric patients.

Another art therapist, working with a variety of groups, summed up his
experiences succinctly: 'I have found that the outcome of a session depends

less on the theme chosen than on what the clients bring with them to the group.'

Thus what actually happens in the group is influenced by many factors, such as:

outside limitations

the setting in which the group functions

the particular client group

the stage the group has reached

current mood and preoccupations

the kind of group and its emphasis on certain issues and ways of working

the style of leadership

the choice of a particular theme or activity

the way discussion is handled

All these factors will have a bearing on the outcome of any one session. The important thing to keep in mind is that you are choosing a theme in relation to your group and its current needs.

10. The Activity

This is the time when everyone is usually totally absorbed in what they are doing. A 'no talking' rule can intensify this experience, which can be very deep. Sometimes it happens naturally, especially with experienced groups. Leaders should try to ensure that there will not be any interruptions during this period (e.g. latecomers, notices about lunch, etc.), as these can be very unsettling and break the 'spell' of deep concentration. Any time-limits should be announced at the beginning.

The activity itself is really important. It is not just the time needed to get something on paper which can be discussed, but a time during which non-verbal processes take over and people are working things out through paint, clay, etc. This process cannot be adequately described in words, and this is why it is important that group leaders have first-hand experience of trying the activity themselves.

There are some groups for whom the activity can promote useful conversation which is to be encouraged. For instance, some adolescents who are usually too self-conscious to express opinions can 'open up' while they are engaged in a group painting, or working with clay. Encouraging conversation can also be important for groups of mentally handicapped adults or elderly people, living in the community but attending weekly art sessions. Here talking and making friends are part of the purpose of the sessions.

The beginning of the activity time can be awkward for some. There are materials to organise, and the leader needs to be available to help here.

Then, when everyone has got these and settled down, there is usually a short hesitant period while people sit and think about what they are going to do. This is fine, and should cause no concern. However, occasionally there are one or two people who are really 'stuck'. It can be a terrifying experience staring at a blank piece of paper, while all around everyone else seems to know what they want to do. The therapist or leader needs to help out here, perhaps with some gentle questions, to draw out what that person feels about the theme. (It may not be appropriate for them, in some unforeseen way, in which case it should be modified or left.) If everyone is stuck, it is probably because the explanation of the theme was not clear enough, or because the introductory period was too rushed. The only thing to do here is to go through it again, perhaps with more group discussion, rather than leave everyone struggling.

People work at very different speeds. Some people rush into things and finish very quickly; others work at a slow and measured pace. This means that people will often finish at different times. Two things can help here: fast workers can be encouraged to do a second painting while waiting, or to reflect in a constructive way on what they have done. Slow workers may not finish (and usually this does not matter), but can be helped by being informed when time is nearly up so that they can decide what is most important.

It is sometimes really interesting to watch how people paint, and see where they put the greatest energy, where they are more tentative, where they wait and reflect. If you are not participating in the activity, it can be very worth while just to observe what is going on.

11. Discussion

The physical arrangements for the discussion are important. Everybody needs to be able to see what is being discussed, and it facilitates group cohesion and interaction if everyone can also have eye contact with one another. Some groups can manage these while staying in the same positions as for the activity, or by standing round the finished work, if it is a group project. Some groups are lucky enough to have a messy painting area and a comfortable relaxation area with armchairs and carpet, so that everyone can sit in a circle with the paintings in the middle on the floor.

Groupwork

Leading a discussion about the paintings produced is another whole group session. As such, there are many models of groupwork available, and it is a good idea to consult some of the books listed in the Groupwork section of the Bibliography at the back of this book. I will outline three of the most usual models used with personal art or art therapy groups. It is important that everyone in the group is clear about the process of discussion that is being used.

(a) Everyone Takes Turns. This is the most usual way of sharing the results of the session, and can be very fruitful. It is essential to say whether everyone is expected to share their paintings, or whether there is no obligation. The therapist or leader may ask if anyone would like to start, and everyone else follows on round the circle in turn; or the first person can choose the next one, and so on; or everyone takes a turn when it feels right. If there is time left at the end, a general discussion may develop.

If the group is large, sharing all the paintings takes a long time, and it is important to allow for this. If time runs out before one or two members have shared their work there may be an 'unfinished' feel about the session for them. The leader needs to decide, in conjunction with the group, how much time each person has, and the method of time-keeping. Sometimes not all members of the group want equal time, and the timing sorts itself out; at other time a formal 'five minutes each' is needed.

The leader can encourage group participation by asking what other people think, so that not all comments are directed just to the leader. If the leader has taken part in the activity, then she/he will probably be expected to share too, unless time runs out. Here the leader or therapist threads a fine line between being and not being a member of the group: disclosing something of themselves, yet not burdening the group with their most pressing problems.

There are several advantages in taking turns:
(i)   For people who have not done it before, talking about their paintings (which may contain very personal statements) can be an exposing experience. Everyone taking turns can help people feel they are not alone, and that 'breaking the ice' is a group endeavour. (However, it is wise to respect group members who do not wish to share their paintings, for whatever reason.)
(ii) In a new group, everyone sharing can help group members to get to know each other through their pictures.
(iii) In an ongoing group, the security of structured sharing can help people to build up trust, and become more adventurous about what they are willing to disclose in their paintings and the discussion.
(iv) It is a way of ensuring that quieter members of the group have their share of time, and that certain members of the group do not dominate the discussion.
(v)   The 'equal shares' aspect of this method appeals to many peer and self-help groups.
There are however, some disadvantages:
(i)   Each person will only have a fairly short time (unless the group is very

small), and this can be frustrating. Sharing in pairs or subgroups can help here.

(ii) The discussion usually sticks fairly closely to the pictures, and sometimes this can be superficial.

(ii) Structuring the discussion can be seen as artificial, in that it removes some of the 'free flow' of group interaction. The safety of the structure is seen as an obstacle to exploring conflicts which may arise.

(b) Focus on One or Two Pictures. Some leaders feel that taking turns is artificial and leads to superficiality. They feel more is gained by allowing one or two people more time than the rest, or using the whole discussion time on one or two pictures. The individuals may be chosen, or choose themselves, because their need is greatest at that moment; others can then be included by asking if they have had any similar experiences. Sometimes the sharing of just one painting can lead to a deep discussion which involves everyone in the group in a very meaningful way.

(c) Focus on Group Dynamics. In this kind of discussion the group is simply available for anything to happen. The result may be a general discussion, or under the guidance of a skilled therapist a verbal psychotherapy group based loosely on the paintings. The therapist may ask if anyone would like to talk about their pictures, and then wait to see what comes up. In a free-ranging psychotherapy group, expression of real feelings and conflicts is encouraged; for instance, if a group member gets angry this may be looked at in terms of projections of feelings about that member's parents or spouse. In this way it is hoped to resolve conflicts felt by group members, and which may have brought them into therapy. Members of the group are encouraged to help each other and pool their experiences. In this model of discussion, the pictures are the jumping-off point; they may play a large part in the discussion, or have a relatively minor role, and rarely will there be time to look at all the paintings in depth.

Therapists leading such groups need considerable experience, which may be gained through training, or by co-leading a similar group with someone already experienced.

12. Interpretation

There are one or two widespread assumptions here, which can be quite misleading. One is that it is the leader's or therapist's job to interpret group members' paintings.

This assumption has its origin in one of the first uses of art therapy, as an adjunct to psychoanalysis. Patients produced pictures in order for them to be used as material for the analysis, in the same way as dream material might be explored using the same theoretical framework (e.g. Freudian, Jungian, Kleinian, etc.). The process of painting them was not seen as important.

This kind of interpretation always takes place in a particular theoretical framework (or psychoanalytical school), and requires considerable training and experience. Art therapy groups of this kind are led by art therapists qualified and experienced in this particular field.

However, most leaders and therapists find themselves working with groups in institutions which have no single therapeutic stance; or in the community, where there is no therapeutic framework at all. It is up to them to choose for themselves the theories they personally find most helpful, and these can range from several psychodynamically oriented theories to the many humanistic psychologies.

The second widely held assumption is that interpretation is based on a knowledge of symbols in a one-to-one equivalence of meaning. This is rarely the case. More usually, symbols have a range of culturally based meanings (e.g. the sun can indicate summer, light, warmth or heat). Most symbols also have a subjective meaning, which can vary from person to person, usually within the range of accepted meanings, but sometimes completely outside it, according to that person's experience.

Working in similar contexts may give rise to symbols with a range of similar meanings, but care is needed to avoid extrapolating too easily from one context to another. For instance, an art therapist in a psychiatric hospital, working with many depressed patients, may notice several black and red paintings. If she/he then sees another black and red painting, perhaps elsewhere, she/he may or may not be correct in guessing that the painter is depressed; there is the apocryphal story of the man who painted a black and red picture and then announced that it showed his relief that his bank account was 'in the black' once more. Obviously the wider experience a therapist or leader has, the more their guesses are likely to be near the mark.

At one level we are all engaged in interpretations: we all look at the world in different ways and with different assumptions about it. This often means that our interpretations of an event or a picture say as much about us and our frames of reference as they do about the matter in hand. Some good exercises to explore this are Nos. 206-208 in Section J in Part Two. While our interpretations might be true for ourselves, we must beware of foisting them on other people.

There is a sense in which a painting can sometimes 'speak back' to the artist, and this is a process to encourage, as it enables people to have a dialogue with themselves. People sometimes need to sit with their paintings for a little while to let this happen.

Interpretation is obviously a minefield where leaders can make many mistakes. Are there any guidelines? The most important thing is how the painter of the picture sees it, and what she/he meant. In an ongoing group, as trust is built up, and people feel safe, they will be prepared to be more open and disclose more information and feelings.

A sensitive leader and perceptive group members can also help someone to draw out 'hidden depths' for themselves, but this needs to be suggested rather than presented as fact. A particular interpretation may be more to do with the speaker than the painter; or the painter of the picture may not be ready to hear what is being suggested. There has to be a tentativeness about any interpretation, and an acceptance on the part of the recipient.

In an ongoing group a woman did a detailed drawing of cracking ice to demonstrate how she had felt when her marriage was 'cracking up'. Several months later, the art therapist was leading a one-day workshop in another town, and commented about a jagged painted pattern: 'The last time I saw a pattern a bit like that, it was about someone's marriage breaking up.' She was fairly amazed to receive the reply: 'Well, you've guessed right first time, I'm going through it at the moment.' This sort of interpretation is intuitive guesswork, based on experience of others and of oneself, and on a familiarity with visual communication.

To summarise, I have listed below some of the possible ways of looking at the group's pictures:

(a) Each person talks about his or her work, without comment or questions from others.

(b) In addition to (a), other people ask questions and make comments. This needs to be done sensitively. If a comment is not accepted by the painter, it may be because she/he is not ready for it, or because the comment is inappropriate: in either case, it would be unwise to take it any further.

(c) People reflect, and see if their paintings 'speak back' to them.

(d) Art work review. It can be rewarding to look back at pictures done over a period of time to see if there are any patterns or recurring themes. Sometimes people can see pictures they did some time ago in a fresh light, and this can bring new realisations.

(e) Gestalt technique. This can be used with any art product. The painter is encouraged to talk about the picture in the first person, and to become each part of the painting in turn. The assumption behind this is that different parts of the painting may represent different sides of someone's personality. For instance, 'I am this tree. I'm quite a strong tree, and I'm well rooted, but I don't seem to have many leaves. It's winter and I'm cold and bare.' After this, the speaker may reflect on whether this rings true for him or her in a wider way. After becoming each part in turn, one can go on to create a dialogue between the different parts of the painting representing different sides of a person.

This technique can be very powerful, so is best used in a small or established group, where there is a lot of trust and support available for group members.

13. Ending the Session

Many sessions are bound by institutional timetables, and it is vital to finish on time. Sometimes the clatter of plates nearby is a very cogent signal! It is good to try to end the session on a positive note, perhaps with a comment that sums up the session, or thanks to people for coming, etc. Some leaders or therapists like to include an ending ritual or exercise.

In a whole-day workshop or a weekend workshop, one way of closing is to have a round of comments on, say, 'What I got out of the day/weekend', or 'The best thing about the day/weekend was . . .', etc.

Whatever the situation, the ending of the session should bring people back to the here-and-now so that they can carry on with normal life. The leader should try to make sure that no-one leaves the group with any problems or worries which will prevent them from carrying on their day-to-day lives.

Care taken in the introduction of the session (see Section 4 in this chapter) will avoid trails of 'unfinished business', but occasionally there will be one or two problems of this nature and the leader has to try to deal with them.

In institutions there are usually plenty of 'back-up' facilities, in the form of other staff and clients to talk to, or the therapist can see a person who is upset afterwards. In community groups this is not so easy. The leader can provide information on other opportunities to continue working on the same lines, but it is wiser to try to keep the group experience at a level that is easy for everyone to cope with.

Finally, there is the clearing up. Sometimes the situation dictates that the leader is left with this, but often helping to clear up can be a practical way for people to 'wind down' and get back to 'ordinary life'. If everyone joins in, it is also an expression of group cohesion, and gives a good feel to the end of the session.

14. Recording and Evaluation

It is not easy to evaluate such a fluid experience as a group art session, but you need to make some attempt at it in order to make progress. Evaluation can be approached in several ways, and some of them are outlined below:

(a) By Yourself. Keep some sort of record of the group, as detailed as you

have time for, or as is appropriate in the setting in which you work. Write down such things as:

(i)   Basic information: date, venue, number of session, clientele, members and leaders present/absent
(ii) Aims for session
(iii) Theme or activity used
(iv) How the group went: what actually happened
(v)   How the group felt: initial mood, emotional graph of the group, leader's feelings, levels of interaction and disclosure, etc.
(vi) Individuals: what work they produced, how they reacted to discussion of it
(vii) Leader(s): what you did; co-leaders (if any): how you related
(vii) Summary and future plans

If you are working in the community, that will probably be as far as is appropriate. If you are working in an institution with a therapeutic orientation, such as a hospital, you may be expected to keep all the paintings as records. If this is the case, it is a good idea to jot down any comments made by the artist (or better still get the artist to do so) on the back of the painting.

(b) With Your Co-leader. One of the advantages of a co-leader is that there are two of you to discuss what happened. This can help you to stand back and see the group in perspective, and is a good opportunity to check your thinking. Below are a few suggestions of guidelines to assess your group:

Were any of these positive qualities present: good feelings, enjoyment, commitment, energy, co-operation, sharing?
Were there any negative feelings, and if so, were they adequately dealt with?
Was there any 'unfinished business', and if so, how could it be dealt with?
How did the co-leaders work together?
What did group members get out of it?
Do they want to continue working in this way?
Looking back at the session(s), was the end-result of the experience rewarding and growth-promoting? (This may take a little while to judge.)
Were the aims of the session(s) achieved?

(c) With the Group Members. In a community or short-term group this is probably best handled by including an evaluation session or questionnaire at the end of the session. In an ongoing group in a therapeutic institution there may be more emphasis on progress of individuals. If this is the case, it can be useful to spend a session with each person looking at their work over a period of time — say, every 4-8 weeks — to chart changes and

progress and formulate future needs. In some institutions, notes are added to clients' or patients' files: this depends on that institution's and therapist's style of record-keeping.

(d) 'Feedback' to Other Staff. If you work in an institution where the art group is part of an overall programme, it is vital to give 'feedback' to other staff, e.g. nurses on wards, doctors in charge of treatment, social workers, other teachers, etc. Sometimes this entails a brief verbal report in a staff meeting; sometimes it means going through the pictures to explain what people have experienced and communicated. This can facilitate a broader understanding of people's problems. For instance, an elderly lady attending a day hospital for depression painted a picture of her sister who had died. Other staff were previously unaware of this, as she had never spoken about her sister.

(e) Supervision/Consultation. This is vital to continued learning and development. 'Supervision' usually has a management aspect to it and takes place within an agency. 'Consultation' is a voluntary process, and may take place independently of an agency or use outside consultants.

Whatever the framework, the task is to learn to improve relevant skills, by discussion of work in progress with more experienced leaders and therapists. If there are few experienced people in your area, a peer supervision consultation group will be the next best, so that people working in similar ways can learn from each other. The content of these sessions can be quite diverse: leadership problems, warming-up techniques, coping with institutions, presenting case material and so on.

On a more informal level, it is good to get together with others working in similar ways, just to share approaches, thoughts and views. In my own city, the local art therapists hold two kinds of meetings. The first (every two months) is an informal meeting for anyone interested in art therapy, at which working conditions, group business and arrangements for lectures and workshops are discussed; we also have an art therapy session for ourselves from time to time. The second kind of meeting (every month) is for working art therapists, who present pictures of clients with whom they are 'stuck', or other problems on which they would value others' views.

If you are using art with groups in a personal way on your own, you may be able to get support from your local or regional art therapists. In most areas there are meetings for art therapists to meet informally and exchange their ways of working and thrash out any problems. Contact the British Association of Art Therapists (see back of book for address) for details of your local contact.

(f) Books. It is worth consulting books on groupwork for a range of

methods of recording and evaluation. *Coding the Therapeutic Process* by Murray Cox is useful on recording.

15. Alternative Patterns of Sessions

Although very many art groups use the format outlined in Section 7 of this chapter, and much of the chapter has been written with this in mind, it would be wrong to suggest that this is the *only* correct way of proceeding. There are good reasons for adopting other patterns, according to the client group, setting, etc. This section describes one or two alternatives.[3]

Discussion Followed by Painting

In this format, much longer is spent on the initial discussion, which is an activity in its own right, rather than just an introduction. This is particularly appropriate for groups which need a long time to get into the activity; for example, a psychogeriatric group, or a group of long-term schizophrenics on 'rehabilitation wards', or some children's groups. After the discussion has started ideas flowing, the group engages in the activity. The final discussion tends to be fairly brief, with members of the group mainly showing their pictures to others. (If group members do not have much 'insight', it is pointless to spend a long time on reflective discussion.)

Some groups do not discuss the paintings at the time of the group, but save this for the next session. The format would then be: discussion of last week's work, followed by this week's activity. Although in general this seems a rather fragmented way of doing things, there can be sound reasons for adopting it. A family therapist using art asked the families he saw to do pictures right at the end of their sessions. That gave him a chance to look at the pictures with a colleague between sessions, so that he could present them positively in the next session. These pictures then formed the basis of the discussion, with another theme for a picture being undertaken at the end of the session.

Painting as Main Activity

For some groups painting or another art activity is the main focus, and discussion is not very relevant. This is true for groups which may find verbal communication difficult, e.g. mentally handicapped groups, some children's groups. Here the importance of the art activity is that it provides a much-needed vehicle of communication. It can also be a deliberate choice for groups which tend towards over-verbalisation!

Emphasis on Social Aspect

This can be important for groups of isolated people who are living in the community, but come together for weekly art sessions in a day hospital or day centre. They may be groups of mentally handicapped, chronic schizophrenics or elderly people. In these groups, talking tends to be encouraged, and activities chosen to facilitate this. Breaks for tea and coffee are also part of the routine.

Another way in which the social aspect can be emphasised is the way preparations are handled. For instance, in a day centre which fosters a self-help ethos, members take part in the preparations of the room and take pride in being included in this.

It is up to the therapist or leader to develop the most appropriate pattern for their particular group; and group members themselves may suggest alternatives. Variations over a period of time may take place, or the group may just wish to 'ring the changes' for one particular session.

16. Group Process Over Time

This section will not discuss group process in detail, as there are many books (some listed at the back of this book) on groupwork which deal with this in depth. It is worth reading one or two of these to clarify your thinking about your group.

In a series of sessions that comes to a definite end, there is a series of stages that most groups go through. These can be described in various ways, from the simple 'beginning, middle and end'[4] to the more sophisticated 'forming, storming, norming, performing, mourning'.[5] In an art group which meets regularly, these can mean:

(a) Beginning. The group meets and starts its activity. It is probably very dependent on the leader to initiate everything at this stage.
(b) Finding its feet. The group gets used to the way of working, and misunderstandings are cleared up. If it is an open group, some people leave, discovering this activity is not for them, or it is not what they thought it was. Others become more committed.
(c) Group cohesion. People come knowing what to expect, and looking forward to group sessions. Trust is built up.
(d) Group members become more willing to disclose themselves in their paintings, and in the discussion. At this stage there is often a very deep sharing, as people openly grapple with some of their most pressing problems.
(e) Ending. This is often accompanied by anger, depression and confusion, even if it is only a temporary break.

An art group has these stages in common with other groups, and it is good to be aware of them and prepared to meet them. These stages are not completely separate — they often overlap each other. To a certain extent they are also present in a single-occasion group such as a day or weekend workshop.

Some groups do not have a definite ending. They continue to meet, ideally on the level of stage (d), of deep sharing through painting and other art activity. Many groups like this have a membership which changes over time, and then each member who joins would go through these stages individually, helped by more experienced group members at each stage.

Joining and leaving can be big issues; if too many people join or leave at the same time, the nature of the group can change quite radically. If the group is functioning well, it is probably best for people to join in ones and twos, so that the ethos of the group is maintained and can be extended to include newcomers. Similarly, people leaving a group can affect the group significantly, especially if those remaining feel 'left behind'.

References

1. M.F. Liebmann, 'A Study of Structured Art Therapy Groups', unpublished MA Thesis, Birmingham Polytechnic, 1979, pp. 51-2.
2. Ibid., p. 127.
3. Ibid., pp. 52-4.
4. Family Service Unit, *Groups* (FSU, London, 1976), p. 13.
5. A. Brown, *Groupwork* (Heinemann, London, 1979), pp. 65-73.

3   *What Can Go Wrong?*

Art groups that take place in 'real life' are much messier than the ideal versions laid out in theory. They are unpredictable because no-one is ever in full possession of all the relevant facts, and therapists and leaders are not infinitely wise. Even if one could satisfy these impossible conditions, there are always outside factors that could not have been foreseen. However, even some of the imperfections can be turned to good advantage, and the resulting art groups can be very satisfying experiences which add significantly to individuals' growth and development.

One way of approaching this subject would be to go through all the aspects of running a group mentioned in Chapter 2, and imagine the effect on the group of the lack of each requirement, e.g. difficult physical arrangements, interruptions, lack of support from other staff, inappropriate referrals, disruptive individuals, inexperienced leaders, bad introductions, poorly chosen themes and so on.

Rather than spell out the consequences in general of these wrongs, I would like to give some examples of things that actually went wrong in a variety of groups. They are taken from interviews with several art therapists, mostly with considerable experience, and working in a wide variety of settings, talking honestly about groups they have led. I have grouped them under five headings which reflect commonly experienced problems.

Outside Factors

Example 1

'On one ward, I arrived to find they were re-decorating the usual room we use. The only place we could go was the dining-room next door; we tried to hold the group there, but other people kept wandering through. It was terrible. We never really got started, and in the end we just packed up.'

Example 2

'Initially staff on the long-stay ward were suspicious of art therapy sessions, seemed not to want their patients to be "over-stimulated"! There was no co-operation and they resisted allowing the patients to attend. However, on seeing the products of the sessions, staff attitudes have changed and they are now keen for them to come.'

Co-leader Problems

Example 3

'Sometimes when staff [in a day centre for elderly] participate in the group, they take over and start telling people what to do, so I mostly prefer to run the group on my own.'

Example 4

'A visiting art therapist got into a confrontation with a group member. It wasn't resolved, and was all left in the air. Later I realised it was up to me, as co-leader, to stop the group and point out that a misunderstanding had arisen over the use of a word which has come to have a special meaning at our centre, which the visiting therapist couldn't have known. I suppose we should have sorted out our roles beforehand; while the leader was in charge of the activity I, as co-leader, could have been ready to clarify any confusions.'

Disruptive Group Members

Example 5

'In one of my groups of elderly people, there was a woman who could not stop talking and other people couldn't concentrate on what they were doing. I tried to control it, but that only made it worse. There always seem to be one or two like that in my groups, and it makes me feel very tense, which in turn makes things worse. I don't like excluding people for that reason because that's what they need help in.'

Example 6

'If someone is known to be disruptive, I don't include them. I used to, but not any more. I also exclude people if past experience shows they will not get anything out of the art therapy groups.'

Example 7

'When Graham arrived an hour late, everyone was at their peak of concentration. He seemed quite unaware of the effect of his entry, and started to talk immediately, so I hustled him into the kitchen for a cup of tea, and to bring him up to date with what we were doing. I asked him not to talk while painting, and not to be late next week.' (Community group meeting in a church hall, see Chapter 4.)

Example 8

'I find it's difficult sometimes to handle one person's particular problem in the group, if it's not shared by others — for instance, grief.'

Strong Feelings Evoked in the Group

Example 9

'I used to think my groups had gone wrong if anyone burst into tears and left the room. Now I think it's their choice, and I don't worry about it.'

Example 10

'Strong feelings can be evoked by some themes; for instance, feelings of conflict, confrontation, loss, hurt, rejection. But if people are experiencing these feelings anyway, I feel it's better to find a way of dealing with them than just to miss them all out, though I would hope to approach them gradually.'

Example 11

'Group paintings are not always predictable; they can sometimes highlight the difficulties between people. But sharing these can help towards resolution.'

Example 12

'I was quite upset by the amount of aggression and hostility that came out in the group painting done by the women's group, in particular between two individuals. Previously I'd had the illusion everyone got on with each other. Later I learned that the two women in particular conflict had met for lunch the next week to talk about their differences, so the group had in fact been beneficial.'

Example 13

'Messy feelings are better than an artificial calm which may be rigid and superficial.'

Example 14

'If all the group members are depressed and turned in on themselves, the group can feel very flat and I seem to get little back. But I think I may underestimate what happens, as sometimes I find out later people have still got something out of it.'

Inexperience of the Leader/Therapist

Example 15

'A lot went wrong in my first year because I was nervous and tense. I was trying to control the group, and appointed myself as its protector.'

Example 16

'Certain themes can be threatening for certain groups, and I have tried to learn to be sensitive to the individuals in the groups, and introduce themes which can be developed on different levels. I have learnt that preparation time is really important.'

Example 17

'It's very easy to miss quite important messages. After a group which had painted early childhood memories, one woman asked me what could go wrong if children had no mother. I answered this at face value and quoted research about maternal deprivation. Later I realised that, as she was a cancer patient, she was probably expressing in an indirect way her worry about dying and leaving her children bereft. I could have kicked myself for the extra burden I had given her. If I had been more perceptive I could have allayed her fears by referring to further research on mother-substitutes. I am now rather wiser about the way people often ask their most important questions indirectly, because it is too threatening to do so directly.'

Example 18

'Two days after learning about the conversation above, someone in a community group asked me how art therapy helped mental patients. Before launching into a great thesis on the topic, I enquired a bit further about what she really wanted to know. It turned out that she had been in hospital herself, and had been worried about her lack of ability to paint there. I and others tried to reassure her about this. I was very grateful to have been able to learn from someone else's mistake, so that I could avoid further hurting someone.'

Example 19

'One of the members of my group did a painting which included me. He was very angry with me, and I realised that I was part of his world at that moment. He was seeing me in a parental role. I had to acknowledge that before we could go on.'

Example 20

'I got into an argument with a group member over his picture of a brick wall. I think he was setting me up. Perhaps if I had used more imagination we might have avoided the impasse.'

Even experienced therapists and leaders make mistakes, as the quotations above demonstrate. This is not the end of the world, providing one can learn from one's mistakes. A good way of doing this is to share difficult experiences with others — co-leaders, colleagues, or people doing similar work in other places.

As can be seen from some of the examples given, it is not always obvious whether a difficult session was a group that 'went wrong' or the beginning of growth and development for that group or individuals in it. A little time needs to be allowed before coming to any such conclusion, and indeed the leader of the group may never know the outcome.

In an imperfect world, there is certainly room for the idea of the 'good enough' leader or therapist, who does his or her best to avoid pitfalls, can learn from them when they occur, and in general has a thoughtful, positive and caring approach to the group and its members.

4　An Example in Detail: The 'Friday Group'

I have chosen this particular example for several reasons. First, it is one I have been recently involved in, so that details and atmosphere are fresh. It is an ongoing group, so that it shows the group process over a period of time, and how the nature of a group can change. It is a group that takes place in the community, so is not bound to any one kind of therapeutic situation (and also has difficulties arising from that fact). Finally, one or two of the sessions (which I shall describe in detail) demonstrate how widely certain themes can be interpreted by individuals.

The group was started by a friend of mine, Heather — a trained art therapist — to explore two of her preoccupations:

(a) colour work; and
(b) the psychology of personal construct theory, as developed by George Kelly;[1]

and to see if they could be related. It was called an 'Art and Psychology Study-Workshop', and was advertised by notices in relevant magazines and posters in suitable places.

The group met on Friday mornings from 10.00 a.m.–1.30 p.m. in a hired church room, with a kitchen next door, where we could make drinks. I was to be initially part of the group, as I was not familiar with Heather's chosen topics, but also co-leader as required. At the beginning I interpreted this as helping the people who came together to feel at home and welcome.

A mixed group of people arrived for the first session. Some had come as a substitute for another workshop which had fallen through, some via posters and advertisements, some via personal contacts. The initial group included a couple practising alternative therapies, two semi-retired women, three women with young children (two of whom had previously taught art and crafts), myself and Heather. Over the next few weeks, during the initial phase, the couple and one of the older women left, and we were joined for varying numbers of sessions by a retired doctor, a playgroup leader, two

47

unemployed men, an osteopath, a woman with older children and an unemployed art therapist new to the city. The attendance varied from two to eight, depending on such things as sick children, visits of relatives and the weather (it often seemed to rain torrentially on Fridays, we noticed, as we struggled in and out of the building with paints, paper, jars, etc.).

Because we were meeting in a church room which was used by many other groups, Heather had to bring all the materials every week in her estate car, which she unloaded while parked momentarily on the double yellow lines of a busy main road outside. She had to bring everything: paints, paper, brushes, palettes, water jars, newsprint rolls to cover the tables, newspaper to spread on the floor for paintings to dry, rags, paper tissues, also books which might be of interest to the group. Heather also had to organise the room each week: take up the carpet in the middle of the floor, bring in some small formica-topped tables from the lobby and put them together to make a large painting surface, put out all the materials (Photograph 1 shows the group at work). Although Heather usually got there early to set everything out, members of the group naturally helped to clear away at the end.

The first eight sessions had a similar format. We started with a cup of tea and any introductions. Then Heather introduced a colour exercise, loosely based on some of Rudolf Steiner's work, using wet paper and water colours in particular sequences.[2] We discussed the results, and then had a short

1: The 'Friday Group' at Work (Bristol Art and Psychology Group)

(Photography by Marian Liebmann)

break for lunch, after which Heather introduced some of Kelly's personal construct theories. The atmosphere was much like that of an informal adult education class, but more personal because the subject-matter was personal, and the group was fairly small.

When the group had settled down, people began to talk to each other more, and ask more questions. Knowing we were both art therapists, people asked us about this too, so Heather asked the group if they would like to try some 'art therapy' themes, which they did.

Earliest Childhood Memory

This was taken together with the first memory of separation, together with 'hellos and goodbyes' in the present, to see if there were any connections between past and present. The results were interesting. Jenny did a picture of herself and her sister being sent off to nursery school. Most of the picture was in black to emphasise the misery of separation.

Audrey painted the occasion when she dawdled on a walk and the others went on without her. She knelt down, bellowed with rage and wailed 'Wait for me!' Her parents must have thought it was funny as her father took a photograph of her, but she was actually very angry and frightened.

My painting showed me visiting my mother in hospital when my younger brother was born, but somehow I couldn't seem to remember much — a lot seemed to be 'blotted out'.

We all found the theme unexpectedly upsetting, as if a lot of our childhood hurts were still all there, if we 'pressed the right buttons'. It certainly convinced us that we had not entirely forgotten our early experiences; and although the 'present-day' experiences did not always dovetail into these, we began to see that there might be strands of earlier experiences still influencing us.

Family Groups in Clay

Heather asked us to model a 'family group'. It was the only time we used clay (mainly because of the practicalities of bringing it, and also of taking home any finished articles!) and one or two people found it difficult initially. Everyone worked away with deep concentration, then we shared our thoughts and feelings.

Audrey

A family group including herself, her husband and two baby girls, with her mother nearby.

Ruth

Three figures rising from a unified base, arms flowing between each member as if dancing or rotating, the balance of the group disturbed by the removal of the fourth member. (Ruth's marriage had recently broken up, and her husband had moved out, leaving her looking after their two young children.)

Tamsin

Four figures on the same base, representing an 'idealised family' she had never known in her childhood.

Jenny

A large number of small figures, lots of brothers and sisters, everyone's children, all coming and going.

Myself

My own small family in the centre, surrounded by a circle of friends who for us take the place of the large family we haven't got.

Most of us thoroughly enjoyed using clay, except for Tamsin, who felt it was cold and clammy. We found it interesting to see that there were many interpretations of 'family' other than our own, and how using clay enabled us to express these in a way that neither words nor pictures could manage.

The Group Membership

A couple of sessions later Heather was away, so I took responsibility for the group for that session. By now the membership had settled down to:

Audrey

A retired teacher doing voluntary work at the local cancer help centre, and very interested in using art in a personal way. She and her husband seemed to have some difficulties.

Jenny

A mother of two young children, she had also done quite a lot of sessional craft teaching; her husband had been unemployed for a long time and was very depressed on account of this. The family was living on Social Security, and Jenny naturally found their situation difficult and depressing.

Ruth

A mother of two young children, and a former art teacher in a secondary school; in her teaching she had been searching for a more personal approach. Her marriage had recently broken up, leaving her on her own with the children, living on Social Security, and having arguments with her ex-husband over financial arrangements. She felt very angry about him, and this often spilled over into other interactions.

Lesley

A friend of Ruth's, in her second marriage, and mother of one child. She was unable to continue coming when she got a part-time job.

Mary

A playgroup leader with grown-up children. She was unable to continue coming when her mother-in-law became ill and she had to look after her.

Myself

A mother of one child, an art therapist and working part time in another job I was trying to leave, and looking for the right next step.

Heather

An art therapist working part time in several different places: a day hospital, a cancer help centre and a school for the mentally handicapped.

Then we were joined by two new members who rapidly became part of the group:

Pippa

A friend of Audrey's and a mother of three school-age children, her main love was painting, which she did in a very lively and vivid way.

Graham

A middle-aged man, whose marriage had split up, and whose son was at boarding school. He had been unemployed for a long time, and was trying to set up on his own, running a magazine about his main interest — astrology. He was a very lonely person, and couldn't stop talking, while at the same time finding it difficult to make personal contact with others.

Because of the newcomers, I wanted to suggest a theme which would help me (and the rest of the group) get to know them, and at the same time be interesting and useful to those who knew each other. So, after our usual initial cup of tea and exchanging of greetings, we sat down round the table and, as we were an 'established' group, I introduced the idea fairly directly, together with one or two other themes, so that the group had a choice and felt they had some say in what we did.

Lifelines

I asked people to draw or paint their life as a line, and include, if they wished, any scenes or particular moments along the way. The line could be any shape, they could use large or small paper, and sellotape extra sheets on if they needed. We had powder colours (Heather was using the liquid paints elsewhere that day), oil pastels and wax crayons at our disposal.

With eight of us in the room, space was at a premium. There was room for four people comfortably round the main table, and two of us got some children's tables out at each end of the room. Ruth sellotaped her paper to the door of a metal cupboard, and Jenny moved from the table to the floor when the number of sheets she needed outgrew her space on the table.

Everyone worked with great concentration for an hour, interrupted by Graham, who arrived in the middle in a great flurry. I gave him a cup of tea in the kitchen, and told him what we were doing. I decided to join in, as everyone seemed to be engrossed and not to need anything; my style generally is to join in unless there are other things that need doing. As people worked, they spread on to more and more sheets of paper. When I saw that some had finished, while others were still engrossed, I suggested that we had an early lunch-break and met again in half an hour. This would give those still working the option of using some of that time to carry on if they wished.

After the break we gathered again. As the paintings were all different shapes and sizes, we moved round the room as a group to visit each painting. They were all fascinatingly different, and for this reason I have included photographs of them (N.B.: the photographs are not all to the same scale). I asked who would like to start, and no-one volunteered, so I asked Graham, who was usually very talkative. After that, we just followed round the pictures in the order of the room.

Graham (no photograph available)

As he had arrived late, he hadn't finished. His lifeline was in the shape of a circle, as he believed in reincarnation. Within the circle he had placed some colours, a house, logs, a lake, which he thought of as 'life resources', and then a grey and brown cell representing his present home life, which he felt was pretty barren since splitting up from his wife; his son was at boarding school. He wanted to take it home and finish it.

Pippa (Photograph 2)

Pippa's lifeline was a meandering blue river which wandered through exotic landscapes, replete with luscious fruits and brightly coloured flowers. Her parents had been diplomats, and had taken her to several Middle Eastern countries, and there had been holidays with Danish grandparents too. The little vignettes along the way showed the Danish forests, a ripe juicy persimmon held in two hands, a little Middle Eastern playmate with black teeth, herself praying in a secret shrine she had made in a cave and her passion for riding. Although she had stuck two pieces of paper together, her lifeline only took her as far as the age of 11. The richness of her picture suggested a particular attachment to that period, and she said herself that in many ways she still felt like a child.

Mary (Photograph 3)

Mary had sellotaped three sheets together. The first three represented her childhood, with rhythmic and uncomplicated wavy lines. The fourth piece was full of energetic whirls and brightly coloured shapes, with knots of darker colours here and there. These were to do with her eldest boy's hearing problems, and the arguments and difficulties with in-laws over her adoption of a child of part-Jamaican/part-Irish background.

2: Lifeline: Pippa

(Photograph by David Newton)

3: Lifeline: Mary

(Photograph by David Newton)

Lesley (Photograph 4)

Lesley had done an ingenious set of paintings in layers to represent her life. The bottom layer was painted in deep blue and purple to signify 'underlying' depression (lower picture, bottom right and left). On top of this, folded in towards the middle (bottom centre), was a layer depicting her childhood (the untidy dark mops), her teenage years (the cage) during which she had experienced a breakdown, and a white cross relating to her involvement with Christianity. The top layer (top picture), which was placed over the other two and also folded inwards, showed a huge white cross surrounded at the top by red and yellow, which she said were good things beginning to happen out of the nothingness below. She had done it in that way because she felt the top layers blotted out the memories of the others — were they gone, or just blotted out, she wondered? Right at the end, she did an oil pastel drawing showing a series of houses, each one progressively smaller. Her parents had moved around a lot, which she had found exciting at first. As more moves took place, the excitement palled, and so she had drawn each house smaller. After the houses came a 'downward spiral' towards the bottom of the drawing, representing her difficult teenage years again.

Audrey (Photograph 5)

Audrey started by drawing her lifeline (on two pieces of paper) as a large light-green spiral, which she said she would really have liked to do three-dimensionally, pointing upwards. The various scenes were significant events in her life, which she had jotted down in the top right-hand corner. The spiral started at the bottom left with her parents and her older brother at Audrey's birth. Higher up on the left is the birth of her much younger brother, whom she adored and virtually shared with her mother. Later followed her father's death from TB (bottom centre), depicted by a black hearse ('Free' was the name of the undertaker) and a sad circle of tearful heads. Further on (to right) were college days during the war (castellated towers with sword, gun and helmet), followed by her wedding. The couple have quizzical expressions on their faces, she said, to signify the difficulties that were to come. In the bottom right she drew herself in her first job as a teacher, both with her pupils and on her own, shouting 'Help, Help!' because it was all too much for her at the time. As can be seen, she had not finished, so took it home to work on, in her deliberate and self-paced way. She also started a third piece of paper, but remarked that she felt the rest of her life was mostly not very eventful. As she was older than most of us, she felt that family life, once started, tended to go on for a long time much the same and turning points would be difficult to find.

Ruth (Photograph 6)

Ruth did her picture in oil pastels, on two pieces of paper stuck to a metal cupboard door. Her art training is evident in her firm and organised use of

4: Lifeline: Lesley

(Photograph by David Newton)

5: Lifeline: Audrey

(Photograph by David Newton)

materials. The colours she used were mostly pastel colours with some strong black lines and shapes. Starting at the top right, the large black question-mark remembered an occasion when, as a small child, she was abducted by a man. This was followed by an expanding bulbous portion, which showed her emerging from childhood. The square shape she related to a need for security, and the grey clouds inside to a period of confusion at college. Black and brightly coloured lines worked their way towards the bottom of the picture, representing an 'unsubtle' marriage, and the two circles, pink and blue, stood for her children. At the lowest point a black cross was followed by a black jagged rift. The cross was for the sudden death of her sister, and the jagged rift for the break-up of her marriage. Both had happened quite recently, the latter only during the previous months. The smallish circles following on from this showed her working through the aftermath and leading upwards towards red and white wings for the present, where she felt she was 'taking off' again, in the direction of the top left of the picture.

Jenny *(Photograph 7)*

Jenny ended up using eight sheets of paper, spread out on the floor, as one thing led to another. Starting at the top left, with her birth (a spiral sun), the line shows her family as an inturned circle. They stayed in the same place all the time, whereas she would have liked to move around. She

6: Lifeline: Ruth

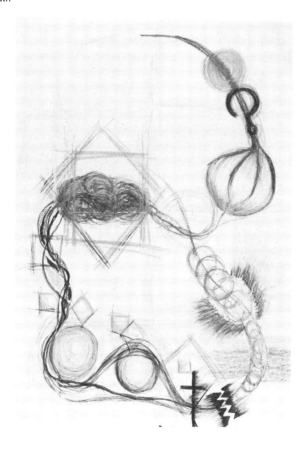

(Photograph by David Newton)

shocked them all by getting pregnant and having her son (small spiral sun) at the age of 17. She thoroughly enjoyed this, and it also helped her to make a lot of new contacts (little people at the top). She then met her husband (top right) and moved to various places with him (waves for a seaside resort, top right), including inner London, where they lived in communal housing with a central courtyard (bottom right) — the best place she'd ever lived. There followed a move to France (bottom centre), where they bought a derelict farmhouse with others, and lived a basic 'self-sufficient' life in hard but rewarding conditions, and where her daughter was born. Then the line led back to Bristol (centre), a time of problems and complications, during which her youngest son was born, and finally finished on the left at the house they bought to 'settle down'. The bottom left flower shape was to represent the future, when she hoped to try to

make interesting things happen from their base, without always having to move on.

Myself (Photograph 8)

My lifeline spread on to four sheets of paper. Starting on the left, the first event depicted is the death of my father (prone figure), followed by a black line for difficult college days. This was followed by the discovery of painting and writing, and a move to London (Underground sign), and then Bristol (coloured lights, a time of many contacts). Then another line joined mine, followed by a red blob (marriage) and a flowering of talents in a new job. The pear-shaped figure showed my pregnancy, and a third line joined us — a yellow one in-between the two darker ones — which twirled around as our young child led us a 'merry dance'. Below this was a black patch of depression associated with work and decision-making, with arrows pointing in different directions I could take out of it. The little figure at the bottom was me looking over my shoulder, harking back to my favourite job. At the right was a green meadow, with flowers — a wish for an easier future.

7: Lifeline: Jenny

(Photograph by David Newton)

8: Lifeline: Marian

(Photograph by David Newton)

We slightly overran our time, and had to hurry the discussion, so that we did not spend as long on the last few paintings as we would have liked. Everyone seemed to have enjoyed the session, and one or two in particular seemed to have gained a lot from it.

We certainly got to know each other and our lives in a way we had not done before, and this helped us to understand each other better. This exercise also seemed to give people a sense of perspective by giving them a chance to stand back and look at their lives as a whole.

Group Painting (Photograph 9)

On another occasion when Heather was away, there were only four of us there, and the atmosphere seemed quite flat and low. I made various suggestions, most of which did not seem to appeal. Finally, the idea of doing a group painting seemed to raise enthusiasm. To start, we closed our eyes and with charcoal 'took a line for a walk' for a few minutes, then opened our eyes to look. Then, in silence, we painted using our 'squiggle' as a basis to turn into anything that suggested itself. Then we moved out to meet the others, and carried on until we had covered the paper, which took nearly an hour. Two of us painted much faster than the others, so that at times we seemed to be in danger of swamping them. The finished result still showed clearly the four contributions, which were as follows:

Myself (bottom left)

Abstract swirls of yellow, orange, red, blue and green, with an intense blue shape emerging in the centre.

9: Group Painting by Four Members of the 'Friday Group'

Graham   Audrey

Marian   Pippa

(Photograph by David Newton)

Pippa (bottom right)

On the far right, she had started by painting a nostalgic scene of the house and garden her family had left a year previously, and which she had loved. She had painted the sun in because children often do, and she still sometimes felt very much a child. Then, without quite meaning to, she had painted two aborted foetuses (bottom left) being plucked out by a long, muscular arm reaching down from above. She had in fact had two abortions — one some years back, and the other one only the previous week — and was still trying to clear her mind about it. She had not meant to tell anyone — the foetuses just 'popped up' in the painting. Her doctor had been against the abortion, but as she and her husband already had three children she felt they had made the right decision. We spent quite a while in the group discussing it, and I encouraged her to carry on using painting to 'clear her mind'.

Audrey (top right, but described from her way up)

She started by filling in the charcoal curves with red, blue and purple, then felt some straight lines were needed to balance these, and painted grey criss-cross lines, which she said were prison bars representing her husband and her marriage. The flames at the bottom left were the fire she was looking for inside herself — but at the same time she was frightened, in case the fire led to an explosion; she did not want her marriage to break up. When someone asked her about the dark blue bird hovering above, Audrey burst into tears and said it was herself wishing to 'fly' but feeling she couldn't.

Graham (top left, but described from his way up)

He started with browns and greens near the bottom, then widened out and mirrored my sweeps of colour and egg-shape. Then he added strong splodges of red (centre) and finally a fence which echoed Audrey's prison bars, and a few trees to make a 'Swiss landscape' (although he had never been to Switzerland).

For most of the group it was their first experience of doing a group painting, which probably accounts for the fact that the individual contributions are mostly fairly separate. It can be quite a threatening experience, in a culture which stresses individuality, to suddenly try to merge with others in doing a group painting.

The whole morning was a very deep and moving shared experience for all of us, and it was quite difficult for us to clear up and go home.

Melting Mirror

This was a 'fantasy journey' led by Heather, in which we imagined we were standing in front of a mirror, which then melted and shook, leaving us face to face with ourselves as children in a room we knew well and liked. What was that child saying to us, and what would our reply be? As we gathered up our paints, it turned out that all of us were 'stuck' as we needed more time to 'get into it', so we asked Heather to go through it again. The resulting paintings looked at ourselves at different ages and places. A few examples:

Ruth

Her picture showed herself taking a photograph of herself, aged three or four, dressed up as a queen, in her back garden where she spent most of her time playing on her own. She had not had a very happy childhood, and this was her escape. The following week, Ruth reported that the image she had painted of herself had haunted her during the week, and she had felt rather stirred up by it.

Jenny

Her main memory was of some very special pink-flowered wallpaper, and the brown lino that was prevalent at the time. This rang bells with several other members of the group whose memories were also coloured by ubiquitous brown lino!

Pippa

She was facing the same way as herself, looking out of the picture in her favourite room — her grandparents' bathroom in Denmark. There was a long arm dropping her on the floor, and the message of the picture seemed to be that she felt she had not fulfilled her early promise.

Myself

I was talking to my eight-year-old self, who was saying 'Come and play outside' in my favourite childhood haunts of old logs and bracken near our house. This too seemed to be an escape from other things in life that were difficult.

Venetia

She was an art therapist with three grown-up children, and had just joined the group on moving to Bristol. In her mirror she was about 12, tall and slim, in a white tennis outfit, in her new room, and wanting very much to be grown up. Now, as her adult self, she felt much more able to appreciate her childlike traits, so there was an interesting reversal going on.

Once again, we realised how much our child-selves were still parts of ourselves. This exercise helped us to get a dialogue going between our child- and adult-selves, and alerted us to needs we still had, but often ignored. It was also a chance to appreciate the positive qualities of our child-selves and to integrate these into our adult lives.

In between these sessions, Heather was asking the group to interpret some of Kelly's theories in paint. For example, aggression as 'expanding boundaries' compared with hostility as 'defensive action'; and guilt as 'discovering you were not the person you thought you were'. We explored these in pictures and discussed them.

Towards Easter we knew we needed to discuss with the group whether the group should continue into the summer. Both Heather and I decided that we needed a six-week break because of other commitments. We discussed the starting date of the next term, and discovered that several people were very disappointed at the idea of such a long break. Our final session before the break was a group mural, which shows some of these feelings.

Group Mural (Photographs 10 and 11)

We all joined in the mural, painting wherever we wanted. Photograph 10 shows the group at work, and Photograph 11 the finished mural. We were using liquid ready-mixed thick powder paints. On the left, Graham's contribution — very distinct and full of esoteric symbols — has a face underground 'pushing up the daisies'. The £40K? referred to the 'price on that person's head', he said. He drew a line to keep his patch separate. Moving towards the right, the blazing sun and grassy bonfire were mine; also some small solid flowers underneath the fire. The tall slender flowering plant was Heather's as were the birds high in the sky. Jenny did a blue shape full of £ signs (money worries) surrounded by heavy black and red lines. Audrey placed herself on the edge and painted a very solid green house (bottom right). Ruth was working at the top right on cloud formations, stimulated by an earlier discussion with Jenny on Steiner's use of peach colour. In between the peach-coloured clouds, Ruth included blue triangles, which she blended into boomerang shapes to link with Heather's birds. She wanted to 'flow' into Audrey's space, but the hard edge of the house was intimidating and she was afraid of offending Audrey. It was interesting to see that later Audrey herself continued Ruth's swirls by making her own dark flowing strokes across her house. Ruth also tried to link Graham's section with the whole of the mural, but Graham quickly reaffirmed his

10: The 'Friday Group' at Work on a Mural

(Photograph by Heather Buddery)

11: Group Mural by the 'Friday Group'

(Photograph by David Newton)

position by going over the line separating his part from the rest. Right at the end, Heather decided to add some insects and a 'can of worms' at the bottom of the picture, seen by others as a touch of 'reality'.

During the discussion afterwards, it came out that Jenny's blue, black and red shape was a mixture of depression and anger at the long break. Several people echoed this, saying how much the group meant to them, and how it was their 'safe space' that was just theirs. Instances were mentioned when this 'safe space' had been spoilt or violated. Some members of the group decided to meet socially half-way through the break, to help them over the time when they would be missing the weekly sessions. Obviously when the new term started, its length and purpose would need to be discussed.

The group mural brought us together as a group, while allowing every-one to portray their individual concerns. The positions taken up by different people demonstrated how they saw themselves in the group, and the interactions on paper showed the group process at work. In these ways it proved a fitting ritual to end the term.

Conclusion

This series of group sessions demonstrates how the nature of a group can change. The group members came together as a class and developed into a therapy group, by everyone's consent. Although no-one was deemed to need the intervention of an institution, most people were at that moment carrying problems of some magnitude (divorce, long-term unemployment, depression, marriage problems, work problems, mental illness, big decisions, etc.) which they were trying to sort out in their own way.

In many ways the problems shared were a typical cross-section of those around in the community at large, and the usefulness of art therapy in the group shows how widely applicable it can be. Heather's open approach, and the freedom to come and go, were most important to group members (in fact, attendance was very regular).

This account may seem somewhat disjointed because it is impossible, within the space of a chapter, to give a real idea of an ongoing group and the sharing of personal lives entailed. It is not an example of a 'perfect' group — rather the ups and downs of an experimental community group exploring themselves through personal painting and discussion.

The final word comes from Ruth, one of the group members, writing just before the Easter break:

> Looking back over the weeks, there seems to be a good deal of significance in the work done on Fridays. I have been working on a large-scale painting at home which begins to link images from the past and from the Friday group. It appears to be a picking-up of stitches and knitting together to find a wholeness and continuity in my life. I am the creator of my life, and the pattern changes as external events or internal conflicts cause me to falter or change direction. Now I am better able to see the pattern of the past, and maybe even the shape of things to come.

References

1. For an introduction to the ideas of George Kelly, see D. Bannister and F. Fransella, *Inquiring Man*, 3rd edn (Croom Helm, London, 1986).

2. For an introduction to these, see Steiner painting techniques in Section 1 of Bibliography.

5   Examples of Groups

In this chapter I shall give some more examples of art therapy and personal art groups in a variety of settings. This is not a typical or a comprehensive selection, but gives an indication of the range of possibilities. The accounts are necessarily subjective, from the point of view of the leader.

This chapter is not designed to be read in one sitting, but rather to be used as a compendium to browse in, according to your particular interest. The chapter is divided as follows:

A. *Psychiatric In-patients*
  1. Admission Ward in a Large Urban Mental Hospital
  2. Small Therapeutic Centre in the Country

B. *Psychiatric Day Patients*
  3. Day Hospital Group Tackling Conflicts
  4. Day Hospital 'Stuck' Group
  5. Long-term Community Support Group

C. *Specialised Day Hospitals and Centres*
  6. Day Hospital for the Elderly
  7. Alcoholics Unit
  8. Day Centre for Ex-offenders
  9. Cancer Help Centre
  10. Children in Difficulties

D. *Staff Groups*
  11. Residential Children's Workers
  12. Staff at a Day Hospital for Elderly
  13. Teachers of Peace Education

E. *Community Situations*
  14. 'Art as Communication' Day Workshop
  15. Women's Group
  16. Mixed Group of Adults and Children

The following describe one session in an ongoing series: 1, 2, 3, 4, 6, 8, 10.
The following describe briefly a whole series of sessions; 5, 7.
The following describe single-occasion groups: 9, 11, 12, 13, 14, 15, 16.

A. Psychiatric In-patients

1. Admission Ward in a Large Urban Mental Hospital

This was one of a regular series for mental patients in an acute admissions ward in a large mental hospital. There were five patients on this occasion, mostly people who had been in an art therapy group before, and were well known to the art therapist, Sheena. The patients included a long-standing alcoholic, an agoraphobic, and three others whose diagnosis Sheena did not know; three were women, two were men. There were also four members of staff: herself, an art therapy student (a woman), an occupational therapy student (a woman) and a medical student (a man).

It always took a while to get a group together on an admission ward because the patients were in a fairly bad way and found it difficult both to motivate themselves to get there and to function well in the group once they had arrived.

The group took place in the occupational therapy room attached to the ward. It was large and quiet, with pleasant posters on the wall, and had a group of tables with chairs round it on one side and a circle of easy-chairs on the other side.

Sheena welcomed everyone, and asked people to say their names and one or two words about how they were feeling. Then she asked them to spend 10-15 minutes drawing or painting anything they liked. There were plenty of materials to hand, and most people used paints, with a couple preferring crayons. While they were finishing, Sheena made some coffee, to help the atmosphere to be informal and sociable.

After coffee, she introduced the main theme: past, present and future, all on one piece of paper. She reassured people by saying that although looking into the future could be quite 'scary', it could be a good thing to do in a safe environment.

Most people divided their pape. into three with lines and worked for quite a long time. When most people had finished, the group moved on to discussion. Sheena asked everyone to turn back to their first paintings, and each person in turn talked about both paintings she/he had done. There was not time to talk about everything, so she made sure that at least all the patients had a chance to say what they wanted.

In general, most of the patients saw their past as wonderful, a state to 'get back to'; their present muddled, confused and unhappy; and their future as fairly bleak and hopeless. By contrast, most of the staff members' futures were much more hopeful. Some examples will clarify this:

Margaret. Her past showed a nice house and a nice husband, and she saw the past as totally rosy. Her present was empty, save for some black clouds. Her future consisted of some grey land together with some grey and black birds. Sheena asked her if a change of colour would lead to a more hopeful outlook, and Margaret said: 'I suppose it could do. When I feel a bit better,

I expect I'll see the future as more hopeful.'

Raymond. His introductory painting depicted a lone cottage with a red roof, in open countryside — a wish he had always had as a child, and never been able to fulfil (his present accommodation, on his own, was in a block of flats). His past showed himself and his wife, together with his four sons and their girlfriends, drawn as stick figures in pink and green, all happy. His present showed himself, and — in a box laid on its side — his dead wife. His future showed himself in pink in a box lying on its side (i.e. dead), all the sons in green, their spouses in black, and then rows and rows of red figures, all the future children. This fitted in with his interpretation of the future as 'carrying on the bloodstock'. He said it was not up to him to 'tamper with Fate', and the general feeling emanating from his pictures was that he felt he had no power to change his life.

Medical Student. For his 'present' he drew himself with huge, outstretched arms like a giant Christ, stethoscope round his neck, filling most of the available space, above a sea of tiny coloured people. When others asked who the tiny people were, he said they were his friends on the course. The group did not quite believe him — they had a sneaking suspicion that they were patients, as the picture portrayed very accurately the enormous power they felt doctors had over patients.

Sheena. Sheena always liked to join in, as she felt that the group went better if she did. Her past showed a heavy panelled door with a brass knob; the door was shut — she felt one could never go back. Her image of the present was herself juggling with several coloured balls, precariously keeping everything going. Life was hectic, but pretty good. Her future showed her firmly on her feet, arms outstretched holding two golden balls, looking happy. When she looked at it again in the discussion time, she and others all thought perhaps it looked a bit static, and her 'present' looked more interesting and lively.

The discussion was curtailed by an over-efficient nurse, who telephoned the room ten minutes early to see if they were ready for lunch. As soon as lunch was mentioned, everyone rushed off — leaving Sheena to clear up.

This group shows the bleakness felt by many in-patients in mental hospitals, and the theme used enabled group members to express this, as well as trying to set their problems in perspective by looking backward and forward.

2. Small Therapeutic Centre in the Country

This Therapeutic Centre was situated in an old manor house in beautiful countryside, and had accommodation for about ten to twelve persons. The patients were mostly between the ages of 18 to 25 years, and were referred there by doctors or other caring professionals. As the Centre had gained official recognition, the patients were able to get their treatment costs and expenses paid by the local Social Security office. Most of them were depressed, but not ill enough to be taken into a psychiatric hospital; some had a history of drug problems.

There were daily therapy sessions, both group and individual, and the patients took part in the general running of the Centre, doing gardening and maintenance work, helping to prepare meals and so on. The art therapy sessions took place once a week in the afternoon, after a long group therapy session, which sometimes ended late.

This particular session took place outside in the courtyard, as it was a beautiful warm sunny day, and clay was used instead of the more usual paint. There were five patients and an art therapy trainee, as well as the art therapist, Linnea. She asked everyone to model a tree out of clay to represent themselves, adding any other available natural materials such as stones, sticks and leaves, if they wished. When the trees were finished, Linnea asked people to place them on a large piece of plywood to create a 'forest'.

When the group sculpture was finished, it was easy to see that each tree was an individual expression of its creator. Some had outstretched hands as branches, others had unstable trunks and lacked a solid base. One was surrounded by an impenetrable ring of stones, another scarcely visible under a heavy blanket of leaves. Here and there, paths leading to neighbouring trees indicated responses to others.

One person, Dan, didn't make a clay tree at all. He made a clay mountain at one end of the board, and then stuck wind-blown 'stick' trees at the top and painted a blue river running down the side towards the other trees, to water them. Finally, he modelled a house on stilts, with a ladder leading up to it, and placed it by the river. His whole contribution was very beautiful, and others made paths from their trees to his 'protecting' mountain and welcoming house. This very much represented Dan who, despite his own problems of isolation and depression, spent a lot of time looking after others; he had a quiet, solid interior that drew others to him.

It was a very successful and enjoyable session, and all the more so because it led to a deep discussion of feelings about where people felt they were, both on the plywood board and in the rest of their lives.

B. Psychiatric Day Patients

3. Day Hospital Group Tackling Conflicts

This was a new group of eight patients, mostly suffering from depression, who all happened to be starting together. They had not done any art therapy before, and it was a long time since many of them had used art materials. The art therapist, Roy, wanted them to bypass the usual inhibitions about 'producing art', and feel a sense of success and excitement from using art materials in a new way. So he suggested that group members should wet their paper, choose a few colours they liked and play around, being aware of their feelings about the colours and shapes produced. Then, if their painting seemed to suggest a definite pattern or image to them, they could develop this image further pictorially if they wished.

The results were very varied. For example:

(a) One picture, mostly yellow, had a thick line across it; how did that person feel about it? It transpired that she felt she had to keep her feelings bottled in.

(b) a painting of cheerful flowers on a black table turned out to be related to the brave front that person was trying to keep up.

(c) A rich picture with a desert, fertile places and a waterfall in the foreground seemed to be linked with feelings and emotions pouring out, irrigating an otherwise barren world.

As people shared their pictures, there seemed to be many unresolved conflicts, bottled-up feelings and simmering emotions, many of them connected with marriage problems. At home, these led to anger and rows, and misgivings as to whether these were justified. When the group members met the next week, they discussed all these things, and Roy suggested the theme: how they had experienced their parents sorting out their conflicts.

The results of these were illuminating. One woman, Shirley, remembered her father being very passive and 'saintly', and not able to cope with any emotion. Her mother had lost a child, and got so distraught grieving over this on her own that she was considered mentally ill. Shirley had never shared this with anyone, and now saw herself as being like her mother, and her own husband cool and saintly like her father. She was frightened at her own anger, and concluded that she too must be crazy.

Another woman identified with this. Morag felt that she could not get through to her husband, despite making wilder and wilder efforts. He was seen as a 'pillar of the community', and she felt her anger must therefore be unacceptable. She had painted herself as a glass cage with horrible things on show inside.

The shared pictures and feelings meant that, for the first time, these women felt they were not alone. The rest of the group also said they felt it was normal to be angry in this situation. Many tears were shed that session, and the two women felt at last that they were acceptable.

Roy felt that the next step might be to explore ways they might change their situations. After discussion the next week, he thought an enabling theme could be: 'What do you fear might happen if you let out your bottled-up feelings?' or 'How would you like to behave at home?' or 'What is frustrating you at the moment?'. Usually people had three fears:

(i) they might destroy others;
(ii) they might destroy themselves;
(iii) nothing at all might happen!

He felt these themes were very powerful ones, and produced a strong reaction in the group. But he also felt that if people were experiencing these feelings it was right to suggest a theme that would facilitate their expression; a 'tea-and-sympathy' approach which ignored this would only reinforce their misgivings about having these very feelings. After all, that was the reason people were attending the day hospital. As an experienced art therapist, he felt reasonably confident in handling strong emotions, and there was further support for the patients at the day hospital from nurses and doctors. He encouraged people to open up, at the same time making it clear that people did not have to expose themselves emotionally if they did not wish to.

This account shows the use of the group, both in checking out each other's perceptions, and in providing support for each other. The themes were chosen to fit into this process and maximise the benefits of being part of such a group.

4. Day Hospital 'Stuck' Group

Not all art sessions give rise to interesting discussion full of insights which promote personal change. Some groups are so 'stuck' that they remain caught in the same old patterns whatever is tried. The session described below is one of these. It took place at a day hospital attached to a large psychiatric hospital. Patients come to the day hospital daily for 6-8 weeks, and undertake a programme of art therapy, psychodrama, psychotherapy, yoga, discussion groups, etc.

On this particular occasion, the group comprised the art therapist, John, and six patients (two men, four women), one aged 20, three in their 40s and two in their 50s. The older ones were suffering from a cluster of problems, such as chronic marriage problems, children leaving home, long-term unemployment, phobias, etc., while the one young woman had problems with parents and boyfriends. John described them as 'casualties of society' for whom there was little hope. Change was very difficult for them, especially as they got older. Our society too seemed to be offering fewer options to those finding life difficult, and John sometimes tried to cultivate an awareness of these things.

This group had been working together for some weeks, and was about to finish its programme in a further week. So John chose a theme (in consultation with the day hospital team) related to the outside world and their future aspirations. He always started with a 'warm up' in which he asked people to paint how they were feeling and, if possible, to include themselves in the picture. Then, for the main theme, he asked them to do a picture containing:

(a) How you see yourself
(b) How others see you, maybe someone close to you
(c) How you would like to be

Everyone worked away for about half an hour, using oil pastels (John had to carry all the art materials from the art therapy room to the day hospital). The rest of the time was spent in discussion and looking at the pictures. It would take too long to describe everyone's work, so I have chosen two of the group, and will describe their pictures.

Molly. Molly was in her early 40s, and had been an in-patient. She was anxious and depressed, and felt her family didn't care for her — only looked to her to service their needs (meals, washing-up, etc.). Her pictures were:

Warm up: chaotic picture of the confusion in her mind, which she felt she could not share with her family, because they were sick of hearing it. She also had death on her mind a lot (her own).

Theme:

(a) She saw herself as boring and black (she was a black woman and had experienced problems because of this when she was at school).
(b) She showed herself wearing a 'nice' mask, which she had worn for a long time when she worked as a domestic. Sadly, this mask was now broken.
(c) She had not been able to do this part, she just did not know how she would like to be.

Jim. Jim was in his early 50s, divorced, and had been made redundant from his job as a sales rep. When he was working, his social life had revolved around the drinking connected with his job. Now he was very lonely, and was disliked by the women staff at the day hospital because he was so lecherous. His pictures were:

Warm up: a picture of a maze, which he related to his attempts to find a job.

Theme:

(a) A thick black vertical band, with a thin yellow one to the right of it. He said this was about his depression and unemployment.
(b) The same as (d). He seemed to have no idea about the effect he had on other people, or the way the hospital staff saw him.
(c) He drew more vertical lines and bands of colour, but these were more brightly coloured — blue, yellow, red, orange. He wanted to be confident, independent and working, with a car, social life and friends. All his hopes for himself were bound up with work, although his chances of finding any were negligible.

John felt very frustrated with the outcome of this group, because he felt that most of its members were the victims of oppressions not in his power to alleviate — such as racism, sexism and women's roles, unemployment, lack of education. All he felt he could do was to help them realise that the state they were in was not totally their fault, and hope that this awareness would lift a corner of their misery and enable small changes in their attitudes towards themselves.

5. Long-term Community Support Group

This group of about ten men and women, aged 30 to 60, met once a week at the local day hospital for long-term support after their treatment as an in-patient or day patient had finished. They were mostly living in bedsitters and unemployed, and felt pretty lonely and isolated.

Heather, the art therapist, saw the purpose of the weekly art therapy session as mainly supportive, to provide some social contact and stimulate the interest of group members. She decided to focus on the world around, especially the natural world, to help them to be more aware of their surroundings and opportunities available. Heather tried to introduce all the activities in such a way that members of the group could relate to them in small everyday ways. This helped them to make a start and also to keep their experiences relevant to their lives.

The following series describes the different ways in which she used this broad theme over a period of several weeks:

(a) Spiral Lifeline. This was an introductory one, to help Heather to get to know the group, and for them to get to know each other. To warm up, she introduced the idea of spirals, and the group thought of examples in nature — such as corkscrews, whirlwinds, etc. Then they drew quick spirals on paper, moving on to a big spiral starting from birth, which they developed to show any important events. Heather also asked them to extend it into the future, to remind them that their lives did not stop at the present.

(b) Practical Group Project. To help the group members feel more at ease with each other, Heather introduced a simple group project which everyone could join in. It was winter; there was thick snow, and birds could not find food. Members of the group spent a long time carefully making little birds cakes for the many birds in the day hospital grounds. The proud moment came when they went outside, placed the cakes on the bird-table and waited to see if the birds would eat them. The day hospital is situated right next to the sea, and before the land-birds could reach the cakes a crowd of large, greedy seagulls swooped down and gobbled them all up! This rapid demolition of their hard work gave them a lesson about nature they had not been expecting, but fortunately they were able to see the funny side.

(c) Winter Colours. As late winter was a particularly difficult and dreary time for people eking out lives in cold bedsitters, Heather wanted to see if she could mobilise group members' imaginations to bring more colour into their world. She often felt, too, that for many people colour was more evocative and immediate than shape, so she liked to start sessions with an experience based on pure colour.

On this occasion, Heather asked people to think what colour they would associate with February. After that, she asked people to imagine what each of their five senses would suggest for February, and relate this to themselves in some kind of poem or picture. The pictures were all very different, showing the variety of associations with February.

Although people's initial reactions to February had been 'How dull!', they soon found a variety of colours and associations. Some chose browns and greys, but others remembered that snowdrops and celandines made their appearance, and added whites and delicate yellows. Someone else thought of the purple of buds preparing themselves for spring, while 'indoor types' built up fires of oranges and reds.

(d) Community of Selves. Heather asked people to think of all their different roles and 'selves', e.g. mother/son/housewife/car driver, etc., to draw them all together as a community. She saw this theme as a way of helping group members to value the roles and skills they did have, at a time when the 'outside world' gave them little recognition. It surprised people how many different roles they could think of for themselves; they also jogged each other's memories as they realised others' roles applied to them too. This in turn engendered a good spirit in the group and a feeling of optimism.

Over the weeks, as group members shared experiences and worked together, they seemed to take more interest in life generally, and enjoy sessions more. They shared problems with each other, and began to make arrangements to meet outside the group. Heather felt they were beginning to learn to support each other.

C. Specialised Day Hospitals and Centres

6. Day Hospital for the Elderly

This was one of a regular series of sessions for elderly people attending the day hospital mainly because of their depression and loneliness, or to give relatives a 'breathing space'.

Karen, the art therapist, always started the session by asking people to say their names, as they did not know each other very well and also tended to forget the names from week to week. She then allowed time for some introductory discussion which often revolved around their ailments and tiredness, with questions about medication and so on. Many of them had considerable problems to cope with, so she felt it was best to allow time for a few moans, before asking them to move on to an activity. Karen felt the choice of activity should give them a chance to reflect on their lives, and how they felt about them.

She liked to use a warm-up theme to get them going gently. This time, she asked them to write their initials and then make a design out of them. After that, she introduced the main theme — their weddings. The resulting pictures and their stories were shared in the group. Here are three examples:

(a) Edna drew a cinema, because that was where her husband had proposed to her. She had also drawn her trousseau, kitchen cloths and towels, eiderdowns — all very practical items. Drawing this picture made her feel sad, as she had lost her husband fairly recently, and was still grieving; but it also reminded her of the good marriage she had enjoyed.

(b) Doris drew a church and her blue satin wedding dress. Her mother did not come to the wedding, and she wrote this down in story form. Her father had given her a grandfather clock as a wedding present, and she had recently given it to her great-grandson, to keep it in the family. Knowing she was helping to create a family tradition in this way gave her great satisfaction.

(c) Phyllis drew herself in her wedding dress, which she had made herself, and her five bridesmaids in apricot-coloured dresses. These were very much things to be proud of in those days, especially as her trousseau (which she had also drawn) only consisted of some sheets and a tablecloth, because she was an orphan. She smiled with pride as she shared her picture, and she also said how different things were now. This reminded her of the many changes she had seen and weathered in her lifetime.

All the members of the group enjoyed it and some came out of the session beaming. They had shared reminiscences of one of the most important events in their lives, and this had brought them closer to each other. This also helped them to remember other events, and they began to look back over their lives with a greater sense of perspective. Karen hoped that, in time, this sense of perspective might help them to cope more equably with their present situations and problems.

7. Alcoholics Unit

The alcoholics unit is a day hospital which provides a six-week programme of intensive daily sessions in group therapy, alcohol education, art therapy, discussion groups, social skills and individual counselling for recovering alcoholics. Both supportive and confrontative methods are used to help break down the denial and defensiveness which are characteristic of alcoholism.

Part of the programme is a choice of activity on a Wednesday afternoon, when clients can opt for woodwork, pottery or painting, to help them learn to develop new interests. The series described below was part of the painting option.

The unit art therapist, Paul, and a trainee art therapist on placement were both available, and they decided this would be a good chance to develop a series together. They decided on a series designed to bring clients into interaction with each other through the actual work, as this would reinforce other work going on at the unit at that time. Below is the outline of the series, with two sessions (sessons (a) and (e)) described in slightly more detail.

(a) Masks of Others. The aim of this session was to prepare people to talk to each other, by starting with something familiar. In the social skills sessions at the unit, people often discussed their 'fronts', their façades which they had come to believe were really 'them'. They were often unaware of their own, but could more easily see other people's masks. So Paul asked the group of seven or eight clients if they would paint masks for each other.

There was great variety in the masks produced. Some people had made several masks to show different facets, or shown a number of facets on one mask. Some had stuck to sunny and cheerful masks, showing the 'brave fronts' adopted by people in trouble. Others had extended this to include contrasted happy and sad faces, as used in medieval drama.

One man had made collage masks by sticking on 'media images' cut out of magazines. An external mask showed pictures of a car, house, wife and children, etc., to indicate a 'successful family man'. Meanwhile, an internal mask of his real self showed a huge cut-out bottle with a monster's face on it, showing the destruction behind the façade. This mask also included a small cut-out picture of a 'happy family' crossed out with thick black crayon.

When these were discussed in the group, what came out was that people could identify facets of others' personalities as a half-way step towards recognising their own traits.

(b) Mask of Self. Members of the group made one mask or several to represent aspects of themselves, both the sides they presented to the world and how they really felt.

(c) Body Outlines. This session started with a relaxation session to help people actually feel their bodies, and where their lines of energy were. Then each person lay on a big sheet of paper, while someone else drew round their outline. The outlines were stuck on the wall, and people filled

in their own in any way they wanted. One suggestion to help them get going was to express any energy lines they felt in different colours. This session went very well, and everyone seemed to enjoy it.

(d) Section of Body Image. Group members chose one particular section to explore and develop into a painting, e.g. one person painted a bird near her heart.

(e) Group Painting. The group on this occasion consisted of seven clients (four men and three women), and three staff, of whom two did not take part because they wanted to observe the interaction.

Everyone started with one colour crayon, which they could 'trade' with someone else later if they wished. One or two people started off very strongly, but later modified their approach as the paper started filling up and they felt they had 'made their mark'. This gave rise later to a discussion of the need for control, which was looked at in terms of alcoholism, where it is often a key issue. The finished painting covered every bit of space, as if the group could not bear the thought of any gaps (this was often true of the discussion groups at the unit too, when clients found periods of silence most difficult). The discussion also covered issues of personal space, and how much people needed their own space to themselves.

Paul and the student felt that the series had been a success thus far. The practical work had indeed achieved a good deal of interaction, and had been enjoyable for most people. It had also raised a lot of personal issues, which had been discussed in the group, and many of these had a direct bearing on characteristic attitudes in alcoholism.

8. Day Centre for Ex-offenders

This example is taken from my work at a day centre for ex-offenders and others with social and personal problems. Members of the centre came voluntarily and chose from a range of activities which included woodwork, community service projects, discussion groups, video role plays, literacy and numeracy tuition, and art — either on an individual basis or in the weekly 'art group'.

Members of the centre played an active role in choosing their activities, as this developed their initiative and helped them to feel worthwhile people once more. Together with myself and one other member of staff, they had chosen to work on a four-week series on interpersonal communication. The 'Metaphorical Portraits' game was part of this series, and they were happy to try it.

There were nine in the group that day — two staff (including myself), a social work student on placement at the centre, and six members (three women, three men), whose ages ranged between 17 and 32.

I outlined the idea: we would all try to draw portraits of all the other members of the group, not as they looked, but in shapes, colours and lines to suggest something about their personality. I was a bit worried lest one or two group members found it too threatening, or others used it to 'get at' the more vulnerable ones. In particular, one of the women was very unpopular with other members generally, and knew it; she was also overweight and self-conscious about this.

We took about 30 minutes to complete our drawings, using oil pastel crayons, and I joined in as a member of the group. Then I suggested that we played a game with the resulting portraits. I held one of mine up and asked the group to guess who it was meant to be. When the group had guessed, I gave it to that person as a gift, and she/he in turn held up a portrait of someone else. We continued until each person had a pile of gifts of portraits drawn by the others.

There were some predictable ones, e.g. I received a paintbrush, and also a series of brown wavy lines (my hair), but there were also some surprises. My co-leader was startled to find that one member drew him as a black cloud, and was worried about him; and on the other hand, the unpopular member received several messages such as flowers, which suggested that others could see past her difficulties and appreciate her inner sensitivity. Just as important was the hilarity and warmth of feeling engendered in the group, all of whom were used to being 'put down' most of the time. The session had been very revealing, but in a gentle way, so as not to be hurtful.

This theme, with several variations, is a particularly rich one in that it lends itself to many situations. It enables people to communicate how they see others in an indirect and playful way; and also to reflect on their part in choosing a particular metaphor.

9. Cancer Help Centre

The Cancer Help Centre provides an opportunity for people with cancer to try several 'alternative' kinds of treatment. Most cancer patients there come from all parts of England and abroad for a one- or two-week residential stay, during which they try out all the treatments on offer, such as the special diet, vitamin supplements, relaxation, meditation, bio-feedback, counselling and art therapy. Relatives of patients are also encouraged to stay and take part in the groups.

There was only one timetabled art therapy group, so the art therapist, Heather, felt the session should open as many doors as possible for people which they could explore later on their own.

The cancer patients attending the centre were very much normal people who had had the ground cut from under their feet by their illness. They found it difficult to have any concept of the future without feeling that they were looking into their own graves. Much of therapy has traditionally paid most of its attention to blockages in the past, but here was a setting where the blockage seemed to be in the future. Heather wanted therefore to suggest a theme which might help them to look at the future again in a positive way.

In this particular session she took the group on an imaginary journey down under the sea, swimming through an underwater cave to come up at an island where they met someone who gave them a gift. She asked people to paint the gift and the person who gave it to them.

The resulting pictures were fascinating. Several of the gifts were beautiful shells or shimmering jewels, which could be seen as gifts of life. In some of the pictures sharks hovered, preventing them reaching the gifts. It was not difficult to relate the sharks to symbols of death or their cancer. In the discussion that followed, some of the group linked acceptance of these gifts with being able to anticipate the future once more.

On another occasion I was standing in for Heather, who was on holiday. There were five people in the group, all in their first week at the centre: David, a cancer patient in his 30s; Tom, a cancer patient in his 50s and his wife Sheila; Tanya and Jeanette, daughters of a cancer patient who was too tired to attend the session.

After introductions all round, and explaining the nature of the session, I introduced another 'journey' theme: 'A journey you would like to make, or one you have already made.' For anyone who did not want to do this, I suggested painting any image that had occurred in one of their meditation sessions, or trying out paint on wet paper to see what happened.

Most of the group really enjoyed the painting session, and stayed a long while to discuss their pictures — and personal painting in general. Tanya and Jeanette had come to find out how to help their mother to start painting, as they felt this might help her to recover from cancer. They painted with enthusiasm, and we also discussed specific ideas for them to try with their mother, when she felt ready. David had painted a meticulous picture of a journey to Cyprus, where he and his girlfriend were going on holiday later in the year (and had been to before). He also painted a second picture — an abstract with much looser flowing lines — and was keen to continue exploring this way of painting when he returned home. He felt the Cancer Help Centre had given him a new attitude and a new lease of life, and was determined to win through. He was a 'workaholic' businessman, and felt that painting and music might be very useful ways for him to relax on his own and discover his personal life once more. Only Tom did not enjoy the session; he had never painted, and could not mix the colours he wanted, yet resisted my offers to help — as if he could not admit to ignorance. His painting consisted of a few unconnected blobs and bands, and he did not finish it. Sheila had enjoyed doing her painting, but when Tom left early, she followed suit.

At the end of the session, everyone helped me to clear up, and I felt happy that I had been able to suggest a possible direction to three of the group. I also felt very privileged to have witnessed the courage and determination of these people who were trying to carve out a positive purpose in the face of death.

These two rather different sessions show some of the benefits of art therapy for cancer patients. It can open doors to personal communication about 'unspeakable' things, and help to resolve feelings connected with these — and the uncertain future most cancer patients face.

10. Children in Difficulties

This was a group of nine 9-year-olds (eight boys and one girl), who were withdrawn from ordinary schools for one afternoon a week because they had family problems and were finding school difficult. The purpose of the afternoon was to give them extra attention and a chance to play. They spent an hour on art activity, then a short while on movement and trust games, after which came a break for juice and biscuits, followed by free play with a variety of toys, games and apparatus. The group had been attending these sessions for five weeks. They were a very active group of children, and quite difficult to handle.

Heather's main method of working was to try to activate the children's imaginations and draw on their rich fantasy life. She usually started with some discussion, leading into a theme by making up stories that led them into imaginary situations that they could fit around themselves.

Family Tree. In this session, Heather wanted to look at the children's family relationships in as wide a sense as possible, i.e. those people the children related to most strongly. She introduced the theme by talking about fairytale relations, using Cinderella as an example to draw out the children's views on 'nice' and 'horrible' relations. Then she asked the children to close their eyes and imagine they were going out to play one evening and climbed up a favourite tree with a tree-house in it, where they fell asleep. When they woke, they found it was morning and they could hear a dawn chorus. But when they looked out they saw, instead of birds, all sorts of their relations calling to them, some climbing up the tree towards them, others perhaps falling out of the tree — and so on. After they had had a little time to imagine this, Heather asked them to open their eyes and paint their 'Family Tree'.

The results were varied. One boy missed the point (or decided to do his own thing) and painted his new toy car. Most of the group enjoyed the possibility of people falling out of the tree, and made sure it was the 'unfavourite' relations who did the falling. All kinds of people climbed in and out of their trees, and the people most important to them tended to be in evidence in prominent positions. The girl in the group painted a big round tree which (Heather noticed) seemed to be the same shape as the picture of her 'Nan' which she had drawn the previous week; her 'Nan' seemed to be the mainstay of her family.

Some children always finished before others, and Heather asked them to do another picture of their own choice. At the end, all the children held up their pictures for the rest to see, and said a few brief words about them. Heather did not probe if they did not want to say anything, and the discussion was usually brief as they were fairly restless.

Silence. This session followed on the week after the last one, and was just before Christmas. Heather had been thinking about the children's need to have a space for something to come up inside themselves, and tried to link it to the Christmas star. Perhaps those who saw the star did so because they had been silent and able to listen and look? She asked the children to shut their eyes for a few moments and listen, to become aware of other senses than their most-used visual one. They found this hard, but managed a few moments. Then Heather asked them to think of things that were really silent. One child mentioned stones, and they reflected that even silent stones might help to make a noise when wind blew over them, rain pattered on them or water rushed over them. Heather asked them if they were ever really silent, and for most of them it was only in bed. She asked when others asked them to be silent, and it seemed that this happened mostly in school and when babies were sleeping.

Then they moved on to the painting. Heather asked them to paint silence all round the edge of the paper, and then to paint anything that came out of the silence in the middle. One boy painted white snowflakes in the middle. Most of the children painted themselves in bed at night in their bedrooms, and one very agitated boy painted his father beating him up in his bed at night, which he seemed just to accept as a normal event in his life.

After the sessions, Heather shared the pictures with other staff there, so that they could be aware of any special issues. The children enjoyed the art sessions, and seemed to appreciate them as a personal space, just for them as individuals.

D. Staff Groups

11. Residential Children's Workers

Heather had been asked to run a 1½-hour art workshop for residential workers in children's homes, as part of an in-service training week run by the local Social Services Department.

She decided that, as time was very short, the best thing was to start them off painting. She pinned up a large sheet of newsprint on the wall, with polythene sheeting beneath, and asked the group as they came in to paint a joint picture in silence. There were eight people in the group. After ten minutes, she asked them to stand back and look at the picture so far, still in silence. Then she asked people to continue for another ten minutes, trying to work all the elements into a harmonious whole. When they had finished, they discussed briefly how it had felt, both the painting itself and having to fit in with other people while doing it.

Next, Heather asked the group to do the 'Family Tree' theme, in the same way as she had asked the children to do it (see No. 10 in this chapter). She explained that it was one which she had used with children, and she thought it would be relevant for people working with children to experience it too.

Most members of the group had related the 'Family Tree' to their families of origin, and this had brought back many half-buried memories. It was quite a powerful experience for them, and they realised the children in their care must also be experiencing similar strong feelings about their families. They were grateful for this awareness, and felt they would have more understanding of the children in their charge as a result of their experience.

12. Staff at a Day Hospital for Elderly

This was a group run by the art therapist for the six staff (all women) before starting sessions for the patients (see No. 6 in this chapter). It aimed to explore the uses of art therapy so that the rest of the staff would be understanding and supportive of the art therapist in her work.

Karen, the art therapist, started by explaining a bit about art therapy, then suggested a warm-up theme: 'Make a circle, then draw something inside the circle and something outside it.' She chose something very concrete so that everyone would be able to do it easily.

The different pictures showed quite clearly what people's preoccupations were. A nurse, who talked about TV most of the time, had turned her circle into the local television-station logo. Someone who had just had her hair done drew a face with a hairstyle. Someone whose car was giving trouble drew a car wheel.

Karen used these to demonstrate how art can bring out things that are on people's minds. She then asked them to do a further warm up, to get used to the oil pastel crayons: she asked them to do contrasts of light/dark, thin/thick, large/small, etc. Although some staff still felt quite strange about doing it, others were beginning to enjoy themselves.

The main theme was related to their work:

(a) How I see myself professionally
(b) How others see me professionally

The results were interesting, particularly as they showed up difficulties between the staff.

Head Occupational Therapist. Her picture was the same on both sides, full of items of her 'practical Occupational Therapy self', such as knitting, kitchen assessment, home visits. She believed in sticking strictly to her role, and showed no emotions to others at all.

Nurse in Charge of Unit. She drew herself behind a desk and higher than everyone else, and said how isolated and insecure she felt. She had only been there a year, and was trying to get new things going, perhaps too quickly. The head Occupational Therapist had complained that she had 'overstepped the mark', so she had retreated behind her desk for the moment, out of insecurity.

Nurse. She drew herself as being very emotional, but felt other staff saw her the wrong way because she said what she thought and felt. She also included practical 'nurse' things, such as injections and beds (even though it was a day hospital). In the discussion, the Occupational Therapy helper asked her where her soft heart was, which made the nurse realise that perhaps she did not show her soft qualities enough.

Nurse Helper (1). She drew herself in a waitress outfit, holding out a helping hand. She felt that other staff saw her as an 'Everready battery' (which she drew) — always ready to be energetic and take things on. She felt she had always to accommodate to others, being grateful to find a job which fitted in with the needs of her children. She was relieved to find that other staff said they did not actually expect her to do everything, and gave her quite a bit of support.

Nurse Helper (2). She drew an outline of a hand with a large wedding ring, also a cup of coffee. She felt more confident at home, and was not sure she was doing the right things at work. Others encouraged her that she was.

Occupational Therapist Helper. She grew quite upset as she saw what she was doing. On one side she drew a rectangle divided into small squares like a games board. In each square she put a differently coloured circle with a black ring round it, with herself at the bottom. She felt everyone was 'doing her own thing' protected by their black rings. On the other side of her picture she drew yellow circles for her home life, which she said was much more sharing.

The session had obviously pointed up issues of hierarchy, role definitions, support, co-operation, etc. Some of them were surprised, and some felt it was a bad thing to bring these things into the open. Others disagreed, and were grateful for the new awareness it had brought. Over the next few weeks, Karen noticed that they all seemed to contribute more equally in staff discussions and when they were working together.

13. Teachers of Peace Education

This was a workshop requested by a group of mainly art teachers thinking about how they could promote peace through their classroom activities. It took place in a teachers' centre on a Saturday, and had been advertised in the peace network as 'Peace Through Art'.

After some difficulty in finding the right room, most of the group arrived. There were seven people, all connected with teaching in some way, and myself. The teachers' centre warden, Steve, had been an art teacher and was most enthusiastic. There was one other art teacher and two former lecturers now running their own workshops. Then there was a teacher of physically handicapped children, and two French teachers, one of whom was about to be responsible for Personal and Social Development courses at his school. We were three men and five women. I had never met any of the group before, but some of them knew each other quite well.

I introduced the session by explaining that we were going to use art as a means of communication, and that — as art teachers — they might find this difficult, or even offensive, if they had been used to thinking of art as an 'aesthetic product'. To relate it to peace education, we would try to look at the 'process' of peace through some interactive work, and see what feelings might arise. We would include work as individuals, pairs and as a group. We used oil pastels as there was no sink in the room or nearby.

Introduction Picture. I asked everyone to draw a picture to introduce themselves, their likes, concerns, lifestyle, anything that came to mind. As the group was fairly small, we decided to share them in the whole group. They were very varied: families, interests in sport, living on an organic small-holding, concerns about peace and the nuclear threat, French flags, etc. All except one (who turned out to have come expecting a lecture on the use of pictures) said they enjoyed pictorial introductions far more than verbal ones, and thought they could say far more in pictures. Looking at their own pictures, they also felt they had learned things about themselves. They thought this method of introduction could be useful for the children they taught too.

Conversation in Pairs. I asked people to choose a colour to express an aspect of themselves, then silently to pair up with somebody with a different colour, and have a silent conversation with that person on a sheet of paper between them. They could continue their own line throughout, or make one continuous line between them until their conversation finished. The conversations were varied: polite and evasive, or friendly and harmonious, or lively, or disconnected.

We shared the results in our pairs, and then discussed the exercise in the group. Most people had found the process fascinating, and also found it interesting to compare the experience with a verbal conversation.

Group Painting. As they had come together as a peace group, I asked them to develop their own view of peace (concrete, symbolic or abstract) in their own space, then move out to meet others, resolving any conflicts using crayons (in silence). Thus I hoped to include the peace issue, both in the content and the process.

The result was most interesting. The picture as a whole was very rich and harmonious, people had worked well together, and been able to resolve any 'boundary' problems without difficulty. The content, however, was another matter. Over half the group members, when they thought about peace, could not think of it except in contrast to war. So the painting included an explosion, a mushroom cloud, a bomber plane, guns and a black CND symbol inside a screaming head. This made people ·a bit despondent, and we talked about the 'boringness' of peace as a major stumbling block to its achievement.

In our general discussion, the teachers said how helpful they thought co-operative work would be in a school system which encouraged individual work and competition between pupils. Co-operative work in itself would be a step on the road to peace, but was very difficult to organise because of the way schools and classes were arranged. The group thought they might make a start by doing some more workshops among themselves. In that way they could prepare themselves better to introduce the ideas and ways of working eventually into their schools.

E. Community Situations

14. 'Art as Communication' Day Workshop

This account shows some of the problems involved in organising events for the 'public', and how these can affect the experience of the day. It also demonstrates one way of constructing a suitable introductory programme, and how to include some flexibility. It is obviously impossible to include many details when there are several activities and a large number of people, so what follows is more of an outline.

This was a day arranged by request for members of the caring professions interested in finding out more about art therapy. It was advertised by newsletters, noticeboards and word of mouth. There were five of us organising it (John, Karen, Roy, Sheena and myself), and we booked a church hall that was reasonably central and accessible. From the reply slips sent in, twelve people were expected, and we arranged supplies of materials accordingly.

On the actual day 23 people turned up! Several people had brought friends, others had assumed it would be all right to 'just turn up'. This posed several practical problems. Our small church hall was inadequate, but fortunately we could spill over unofficially into a larger (but cold) hall next door for the painting sessions, returning to our hall for discussion.

Obviously we could not do any significant sharing in a group of 23, so we divided into four smaller groups for most exercises, with one of the organisers in each group (the fifth one 'floated' to help sort out the many small practicalities). Even so, the small groups were too near each other during the discussions, and found themselves seriously distracted by the other groups.

Other practical problems manifested themselves too. Receiving money from several extra people took time; coffee had to be staggered to avoid long queues and waste of precious group time; and we ran out of paper at lunchtime and had to obtain more.

These unforeseen difficulties meant that the physical arrangements of the day assumed a much larger role than usual in determining people's experience. It was very difficult for anyone to get to know each other, both because of the daunting number and because the inadequate facilities did not allow for relaxing over coffee, for instance.

Nevertheless, everyone cheerfully made the best of it and joined in the programme as far as was physically possible. As leaders, we took turns to introduce the different exercises in the programme, which is listed below. One or two exercises are described in slightly greater detail.

Programme of the Day

(a) Introductions to the day and to the leaders.

(b) Name game, everyone in a large circle (rather squashed), throwing a bean bag to someone and calling out their name.

(c) Introductory paintings. People introduced themselves on paper, then shared their pictures in small groups.

(d) Coffee (staggered).

(e) Conversation in crayon (see No. 13 in this chapter for detail, and Photograph 12). I found myself paired with John, and we had a slightly difficult time following each other round the paper. John felt he was trying to accommodate me, and then felt trapped by this; I felt I was having to take most of the initiative, and got tired of the responsibility. We both realised that these were patterns we slipped into in our day-to-day lives.

12: Conversation in Crayon — 'Art as Communication' Day Workshop

(Photograph by David Newton)

(f) 'Round Robin' drawings. We started with something to symbolise our-selves, then passed our picture on to the next person to add something, and so on, until we got ours back again. One person in the group had drawn little anchors on several pictures. Although she said she was enjoying her present freedom and lack of plans, John wondered if her anchors showed that she was after all looking for a way of tying herself down. She looked at the pictures thoughtfully and said 'Hmm — you could be right'.

(g) Lunch. We put everyone's food out to be shared, and people sat in small groups to eat it, or went for a breath of fresh air.

(h) Choice of five different activities:

    (i)   individual work;
    (ii)   collage;
    (iii) colour exploration on wet paper;
    (iv) group 'mandala';
    (v)   metaphorical portraits.

We had all prepared one activity, but felt we could be flexible, so gave people a completely free choice. Almost everyone opted for one of the last three, and we had to run two 'mandala' groups.

Group Mandala. John was leading one of the two groups. On a huge piece of paper he drew a circle divided into slices, one for each person. He asked people to put whatever they wished in their space, including themselves if appropriate. It was up to them whether to demarcate their territory very definitely, or to blend in with their neighbours, or to venture into others' territories.

Most people first used their space to do a personal picture. Although there were great contrasts, the completed picture seemed to have a whole-ness about it. While two people chose to stick firmly to their own spaces, others were more adventurous and this resulted in more communication. Some were surprised at what they had learned about themselves: one woman, for instance, painted a grey volcano and then recognised how potentially explosive she actually felt. Another person found the negotia-tion of boundaries unexpectedly tension-producing. For most people it was the first time they had attempted anything like this, and they felt it had been a most interesting session.

Metaphorical Portraits. I asked people to tear up a large sheet into eight small pieces and to draw 'metaphorical portraits' of each other, e.g. we might draw someone as a 'closed book', or just an abstract series of coloured lines. When we had finished we played a guessing game with the portraits (see No. 8 in this chapter). As most of the group (with a few exceptions) did not know each other, we were rather hesitant and polite. Two people in the group received sets of consistent images — one of mostly blue-green self-contained shapes, the other of tall and closed-in objects. At the end, one person said how perceptive some of the drawings had been, considering our slight knowledge of each other. Photograph 13 shows the

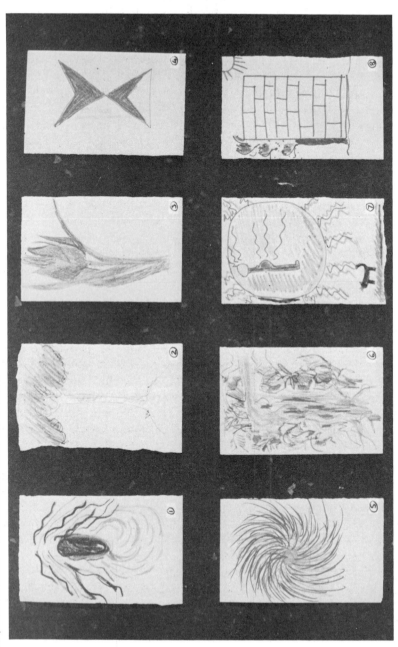

13: Metaphorical Portraits — 'Art as Communication' Day Workshop

(Photograph by David Newton)

set of portraits I took home. Numbers 1, 2, 3 and 4 mostly refer to physical characteristics: my hair, height and the colour of clothes I was wearing that day. Numbers 5, 6 and 7 refer to being seen as having a lot of energy: a revolving Catherine-wheel, a waterfall, warm vibrations. The brick wall in No. 8 was done by the one person in the group whom I knew, and with whom I had had some difficulty in communication because of particular circumstances. She had experienced me as 'impenetrable', like a brick wall. Now, meeting at the workshop, she felt things were improving a little, as shown by the sun in the corner and the little green tree just poking out. My drawing of her, in turn, was a spiky, angular shape — which was how I had experienced her. It was useful to have these drawings to start talking to each other, and we were able to heal the rift between us.

All the groups came together for a few minutes at the end, and we each said what the day had meant for us. Everyone was very tired, but also very positive about the day, and asked when the next one would be! Most people felt they had begun to explore themselves and others in a new way, and wanted to continue that process.

Finally, we cleared up the paints, crayons and paper, and wiped paint marks off the floor, etc. We were very grateful for a helpful and understanding caretaker!

15. Women's Group

The women's group was an established group of twelve women who had been meeting every fortnight for about eight months. It had intended to be a women's peace group, but as many of the women in the group were in the midst of difficult marriages or break-ups, considerable time was spent sharing these problems. Members of the group also saw personal exploration and consciousness-raising as relevant to the long-term pursuit of peace. As there was wide experience within the group, we took it in turns to lead sessions on different ways of working. On this occasion it was my turn to introduce a painting evening.

I introduced the group by talking about the use of art for communication rather than to produce beautiful pictures. Any mark could be a valid contribution, and there was no obligation to join in. I suggested that we should try not to talk while we were drawing. I had brought with me paper and oil pastels, as the only room large enough for a painting evening happened also to be carpeted. We did three exercises:

(a) Individual pictures on 'How I'm feeling', 'Where I'm at', to bring us into the present. We shared these in pairs, and they were so productive that (with hindsight) we could well have spent longer on them. Fiona, for instance, drew an anguished red bird with one head looking down towards 'hungry beaks' (her children) and another head held up higher and looking beyond its cage (her marriage) towards freedom and the sun.

(b) 'Round Robin' pictures. We all numbered our papers with a different

number, then spent two minutes drawing a quick picture. We then passed them on to the next person, who added something for one minute, and so on, until we got our own back. Finally, we had two minutes to put any finishing touches on our own.

Photograph 14 shows one of these. While most people in the group had been trying to add things that were in keeping with what was already there, Zoe felt we were all being 'too nice'. When it was her turn, she added something to shock the rest of us a bit — or give us something to think about. In this picture she put in the mountaineer scaling black mountains, and the thick black clouds at the top.

When we discussed our reactions to receiving back our own pictures, several people were thrilled at how they had been developed into interesting and beautiful pictures from their starting point. However, they were mostly quite upset at the black clouds and pointing fingers Zoe had put in. They experienced it as destructive and damaging. We spent a bit of time discussing how the same marks could be interpreted in so many ways, and the possible misunderstandings that could arise from this.

(c) Group picture. I suggested that we should 'make a base' for ourselves by drawing on the paper in front of us, then move out from our drawing to meet others on the paper, trying to be sensitive to them (bearing in mind what had happened in the last exercise).

The result is shown in Photograph 15. The top of the picture looks fairly harmonious, with people finding ways of accommodating each other, even though some felt a little squashed. The bottom left, however, shows another story. Fairly soon after the start, Diana demarcated a large space in front of her in red crayon (bottom centre). Zoe and Wendy in the corner next to her tried to make contact with her by moving towards her boundary. Perhaps influenced by the previous exercise, Diana interpreted these

14: 'Round Robin' Drawing — Women's Group

(Photograph by David Newton)

advances as aggression, and first strengthened her boundary (top left corner of rectangle) and then withdrew to a small 'inner sanctum' (middle of rectangle). Finally, when they persisted, Diana reached out in exasperation and marked a large black cross on one of their patches. Fiona, further up the paper, tried to 'soften the blow' by decorating the cross, but it was too late. The rest of the group looked on aghast at the conflict the painting had shown up. Several women were not sure how to react at all. Afterwards we discussed our misinterpretations and talked about boundaries and their effect on fear and aggression. Did a boundary show a delineated space, or a claimed territory? The last word came from Zoe, who couldn't resist the pun 'Yes, it's difficult to draw the line!'

The evening had been a thought-provoking one, leaving several of us feeling a bit raw. Later I learned that Zoe and Diana had met for lunch to share their differences, and had had a fruitful discussion. They felt the group painting had enabled them to do this. And at a later date the group decided to use further art techniques to help with communication.

The main use of art for this group was to help the group communicate

15: Group Picture — Women's Group

(Photograph by David Newton)

better by introducing a non-verbal means of communication. By using group interaction techniques, a conflict which had been simmering for some time came into the open and could then be dealt with.

16. *Mixed Group of Adults and Children*

A church-group annual party, attended by about 50 people (age range 2 yrs to 70+) was the occasion for an art activity with an opportunity for playfulness and imagination.

After tea, the adult leading the activity asked people to form seven groups, each group to contain some adults and some children. He gave each group a large envelope containing a large sheet of paper, some sticky paper squares, sticky shapes, sheets of tissue paper, drinking straws, paper hole strengtheners, coloured sellotape, etc. Each group was asked to make something with the materials to do with transport. There were no scissors or knives.

This meant that the groups had to work co-operatively to produce something, and involve all the people in the group, some of whom were elderly and had to remain on chairs, and some of whom were young children who needed help from adults to participate. There was a busy hum of activity for the next 20 minutes.

Some of the finished articles are shown in Photograph 16: a ship, a steam-roller, a helicopter and a three-dimensional hot-air balloon. Every-

16: Transport Collages — Mixed Group of Adults and Children

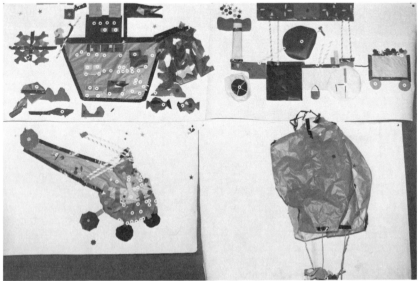

(Photograph by Heather Buddery)

one was very thrilled to see the imaginative results, and the children especially appreciated being able to take part in an activity on an equal footing with adults. Some of the adults, too, enjoyed an activity they rarely had an opportunity to do, and welcomed the fact that it was a co-operative venture.

Although used here as a party game, this activity required participants to develop interaction skills such as co-operation and sensitivity to others, in an imaginative way. These are all vital qualities in most life contexts.

Acknowledgements

I would like to thank the following art therapists for spending time with me, talking about their work, for this chapter:

Sheena Anderson (admission ward — No. 1)

Heather Buddery (long-term support group — No. 5; Cancer Help Centre — No. 9; children — No. 10, children's workers — No. 11)

Paul Curtis (alcoholics unit — No. 7)

Karen Lee Drucker (elderly — No. 6; staff working with elderly — No. 12)

John Ford (day hospital — No. 4)

Linnea Lowes (therapeutic centre — No. 2)

Roy Thornton (day hospital — No. 3)

6 Working with Different Client Groups

The previous chapter gives several examples of the use of different activities and themes with a selection of client groups. However, this book is not the place for a detailed discussion of the needs of all possible client groups. Leaders and therapists are well advised to read about and attend courses on the characteristics and needs of their clients; there are many sources of information on these topics. Further information on art therapy with some client groups may be found in *Art as Therapy* edited by Tessa Dalley (Tavistock, London/Methuen, New York, 1984).

To avoid repetition, the themes, games and exercises in Part Two are not arranged in terms of client groups. Most themes are suitable for many groups, especially if they are used flexibly, and adapted to meet particular needs.

This chapter consists of short notes on some client groups, related to their participation in personal art activities. If a particular section of themes in Part Two is recommended for a client group, this does not mean that other sections are unsuitable — it is up to the leader to look at the particular needs of the group. This chapter is divided into two parts:

A. Those in Institutions
B. Those Attending Day Facilities

A. Those in Institutions

1. Psychogeriatrics in Mental Hospitals

These are elderly people who can no longer live in the community, and may be suffering from senility, confusion, wandering, incontinence, etc. For them, group art sessions will often concentrate on 'reality orientation' and activities which help them maintain their concentration on day-to-day tasks so that they remain able to cope with as many practicalities as they are able. For some, it may also be helpful to include activities which help them to remember their achievements, and give them a sense of dignity (see also No. 6 of this chapter — Elderly People).

*Recommended Sections:** D. Concentration, Dexterity and Memory
E. General Themes

2. Chronic Schizophrenics

These are often people who were admitted to hospital many years ago, for reasons for which no-one would be admitted today. Some of them may be in the process of rehabilitation to a state in which they may be able to live outside the hospital, with plenty of support. Others have made their lives in the hospital and will never leave. They often enjoy art, but tend to repeat the same 'motif' many times, or can only engage in limited activities. Some will need the same activities as psychogeriatrics, but some will be capable of more, and activities to expand their skills and imagination can be relevant. These often work well if associated with a special event, such as a hospital trip.

Recommended Sections: C. Media Exploration

D. Concentration, Dexterity and Memory

E. General Themes

A few simpler ones from other sections, such as:

F. Self-perceptions, e.g. No. 110 — Wishes

I. Group Paintings, e.g. No. 189 — Contributions

(See also 'Art Therapy with Long-Stay Residents of Psychiatric Hospitals' by Suzanne Charlton in *Art as Therapy*, edited by Tessa Dalley).

3. Acute In-patients

This group includes patients with a vast variety of labelled diseases and difficulties, such as depression, hysteria, psychosis, schizophrenia, anorexia — to name but a few. Often they will all find themselves in the same art therapy group, and the art therapist may not even know the official diagnosis of each patient. Generally speaking, any of the themes which are not too 'personally demanding' could be suitable. If there is a new group of in-patients, it can be useful to ask them to focus on the events which led up to their admission, e.g. 'How I came to be here'. Therapists working with anorexics may find 'body image' themes useful (although not all agree on this), and may even use these to invent more of their own (see also chapter 'The Use of Art Therapy in the Treatment of Anorexia Nervosa' by June Murphy in *Art as Therapy*, edited by Tessa Dalley). It is worth remembering that some in-patients are not in hospital of their own choice, and may be resistant to any suggested activities. Even if this is not a problem, many are in a fairly bad way and find it difficult to engage in a group.

Recommended Sections: C. Media Exploration

F. Self-perceptions

Some chosen with care from:

I. Group Paintings

J. Group Games

L. Links with Other Expressive Arts

---

*Letters are cross-references to sections in Part Two of this book.

4. Prisoners

Prisoners comprise a broad range of people, with all kinds of abilities and disabilities. However, the security measures and surveillance in the atmosphere of a closed institution militate against any trust being built up. Most inmates survive the pressures of prison by protecting themselves within an outer 'shell'. Any personal art or art therapy will probably have to be done under the 'art' label, possibly in an educational class, and will have to overcome the image of 'chocolate-box' art prevalent in prison. It is best to work in a supportive way, and to avoid work on deep personal problems as this could be too stressful in a prison environment.

However, from time to time there are experimental projects and pre-release courses which aim to broaden prisoners' awareness of problems and opportunities when they return to the outside world. Many of these courses aim to build up trust in the group and use a variety of structured groupwork techniques, and several of the themes in this book could be relevant — as well as ones specially devised for their situation.

Recommended Sections: C. Media Exploration
E. General Themes
F. Self-perceptions (adapted)
Pre-release courses might also try some of:
J. Group Games
(See also 'Art Therapy in Prisons' by Joyce Laing in *Art as Therapy*, edited by Tessa Dalley).

5. Mentally Handicapped

Mentally handicapped people in hospitals are often in large institutions with a multiplicity of rules which, as well as being the only way to cope with large-scale organisational problems, is seen by staff as giving patients a sense of security. Personal art work may conflict with this sort of ethos, especially if it emphasises individuality and exploration. Special care is also needed to ensure that different disciplines co-operate with each other, and give the same 'message' to patients. However, art may open avenues for natural spontaneity and creativity, which can have many personal benefits. Reflection on the results will, of course, be less important than for many other groups. Care may be needed to find the best medium to use (e.g. wax crayons are easy to use, do not break and last a long time).

Recommended Sections: C. Media Exploration
D. Concentration, Dexterity and Memory
There is also a chapter on 'Art Therapy for People Who Are Mentally Handicapped' by Janie Stott and Bruce Males in *Art as Therapy*, edited by Tessa Dalley.

B. Those Attending Day Facilities

6. Elderly People

Elderly people referred to day hospitals and centres for help often need more structure than at earlier times in their lives, as their problems (loneliness, bereavement, failing health, inability to cope with new developments, etc.) make them insecure. They naturally tire quickly, so that groups should, if possible, be held in the morning. Regard needs to be paid to the timetable, e.g. transport, mealtimes, etc. Attention is needed to accommodate all sorts of disabilities such as deafness, failing eyesight, arthritis, etc. Some of these can be overcome with thoughtful seating arrangements, magnifying glasses, good lighting, large brushes and crayons, etc. (see also section on Physically Handicapped — No. 8 of this chapter).

An art group can help elderly people to reminisce and talk about their lives, the unhappy and the happy things that have happened to them, so that they can celebrate their achievements (e.g. coming through the wars and the Depression), see their lives in perspective and maintain a sense of dignity. The group can also celebrate current strengths and increase social interaction.

Recommended Sections: E. General Themes
F. Self-perceptions, especially No. 99 — Life Review
A few of the following section:
I. Group Paintings, e.g. No. 189 — Contributions

7. Cancer Patients and Terminally Ill

In present-day psychology we are used to looking for reasons in our past to explain present problems. However, cancer patients face a blockage in the future, and this needs to be recognised. Themes which help them to face their uncertain future may be useful here.

Those who are actually terminally ill need an accepting attitude and an honest approach to the topic of death, which is a taboo subject in our culture. They may be able to use art to express their feelings and come to terms with death.

Recommended Sections: E. General Themes
K. Guided Imagery, Dreams and Meditations
Some themes in the following sections may also be suitable:
F. Self-perceptions, e.g. Nos. 91, 99, 100, 109, 110
(See also 'Art Therapy with the Elderly and the Terminally Ill' by Bruce Miller in *Art as Therapy*, edited by Tessa Dalley).

8. Physically Handicapped

There are two aspects to consider here. The first is that of overcoming sheer practical difficulties, e.g. transport to the session, arranging wheelchairs, making suitable paint-holders, using large brushes and crayons if appropriate.

People in wheelchairs can even be enabled to take part in a group painting if brushes are tied to sticks and the paper is on the floor or the ground outside! Just arranging things so that a physically handicapped person can use paint or clay may do wonders for their self-esteem and feeling of being a normal human being.

However, some people's physical disabilities prevent them from achieving the results they hope for, and they become very frustrated. Here it is important to try to utilise the physical disability itself to give a sense of achievement. For instance, an engineer who had suffered a stroke was using background washes and felt-tip pens to build up a picture, but was very upset when he could not achieve the straight lines he wanted and remembered from engineering drawings. The art therapist helped him to appreciate the new delicacy achieved by the fragile lines, and he went on to display his work at an exhibition of handicapped artists.

Recommended Sections: C. Media Exploration
                         E. General Themes
Some of the following: F. Self-perceptions
                         I. Group Paintings

Two organisations which may be able to help physically handicapped people to paint are *Conquest* and *Shape* (addresses at the back of this book).

9. Blind

Blind people can take part in art groups, if special regard is paid to their needs. This means concentrating on tactile media such as clay, junk, textiles, etc.
Recommended Sections: please refer to the Media Notes (Section M in Part Two) for themes which involve the use of collage, clay and other three-dimensional materials.

10. Mentally Handicapped

Mentally handicapped people in the community are able to cope with more than those living in hospitals. Suitable activities can be ones relating to themselves and the world around them. See also Children (section 11 of this chapter).
Recommended Sections: C. Media Exploration
                         D. Concentration, Dexterity and Memory
                         E. General Themes
Some simpler themes from other sections, such as:
                         F. Self-perceptions, e.g. No. 110 — Wishes
                         I. Group Paintings, e.g. No. 189 — Contributions
                         L. Links with other Expressive Arts, e.g. No. 282 —
                             Painting to Music

11. Children

Activities particularly suitable for children are ones which provide starting points for their natural imagination and fantasy. This can also be related to the outside world, and how they see it.

Recommended Sections: C. Media Exploration

E. General Themes

Many themes in other sections are also suitable for children, and for some themes children's variations are listed. Some examples:

D. Concentration, Dexterity and Memory, e.g. No. 51 Map-making

F. Self-perceptions, e.g. No. 84 — Life-size Self-portraits

G. Family Relationships, e.g. No. 135 — Family Relations Through Play

H. Working in Pairs, e.g. No. 159 — Winnicott Squiggles

I. Group Paintings, e.g. No. 184 — Group Murals on Themes

J. Group Games, e.g. No. 219 — Animal Consequences

K. Guided Imagery, Dreams and Meditations, e.g. No. 229 — Magic Carpet Ride

L. Links with Other Expressive Arts, e.g. No. 266 — Action and Conflict Themes

12. Adolescents

Adolescents are often painfully aware of themselves, and frequently lacking in confidence, despite occasional bravado. They need the opportunity to try out their ideas and opinions without feeling judged. Many adolescents find dramatic themes catch their interest and help them to find a form of release.

Recommended Sections: E. General Themes, especially Nos. 77 and 78

Many themes from other sections will also be suitable, as for Children (No. 11 of this chapter), and adolescents may be able to use a wider selection from some sections.

13. Family and Marital Therapy

Here family dynamics are important, as well as the needs of individual members. Thus, many of the personal themes will be relevant for the latter, and pair and group activities for the former. For families with problems, art activities may also be a source of shared pleasure which may have been lacking for some time.

Recommended Sections: Family Dynamics — G. Family Relationships

H. Working in Pairs

I. Group Paintings

J. Group Games
Individual Needs —   F. Self-perceptions

If children are involved, see also themes for Children (No. 11 of this chapter).

14. Psychiatric Day Patients/Clients Attending Day Hospitals or Day Centres

A wide variety of themes will be relevant here, depending on the nature of the group and the particular needs. They may include very different kinds of people, capable of different levels of insight, and the choice of theme will need to be varied accordingly. Day psychiatric patients go home at night, and are therefore more active than in-patients in outside activities and relationships; these can be used as material for art groups.

Recommended Sections: All, bearing in mind the needs of each group and the individuals in it.

15. Probation Clients

Offenders, too, include a vast range of people with different needs and abilities. Again, levels of insight will vary, and the choice of theme or activity should be tailored to the group's needs.

Recommended Sections: All, bearing in mind the needs of each group and the individuals in it.

16. Alcoholics

Most of the comments in the previous section apply. Many alcohol treatment centres, as well as helping people to develop personally, also try to look at the pattern of events that leads up to drinking, and at some of the issues associated with it.

Recommended Sections: All, bearing in mind the needs of the group and the individuals in it.

17. Professionals

This 'group' would include any members of caring professions, such as art therapists, teachers, social workers, youth leaders, church workers. They can usually be assumed to have a fair degree of insight, but may not have used art materials before. Often they are particularly interested in the more deeply personal and group themes; it depends very much on the purpose of their session.

Recommended Sections: All (except Sections D and E, which will probably not be relevant). Some may have a particular interest in: F. Self-perceptions.

18. General Public

This includes almost everyone. The only thing that can be said with any certainty is that the leader may have very little idea beforehand about any problems members of the group may have. This means being fairly cautious in the choice of theme, and avoiding very personal ones until the group is better known. It is one thing uncovering a big problem, and quite another dealing with it. It is best to keep the level of activity fairly light, and themes which can be interpreted on many levels are useful here.

Recommended Sections: All, but avoiding themes which are very personal.

19. Other Special Groups

There are many other special groups and subgroups not mentioned here, e.g. drug addicts, agoraphobics, women's groups, men's groups, ethnic minority groups, protest groups, self-help groups of all kinds ... the list could never be complete. The main thing is to work out what their needs are, and attempt to meet them.

PART TWO

THEMES, GAMES AND EXERCISES

Introduction

Apart from a few physical and verbal 'warm-up' games, this collection includes only art activities. Leaders and therapists who want to make substantial use of games, movement, verbal, drama, music or other activities should consult one of the more specialised books on that particular area. There is a Bibliography at the end of this book which contains many of the better-known titles.

This is not to say that art activities should be used in isolation; on the contrary, they work well alongside other expressive arts, and many groups use several means of expression in the same session or over a series of sessions.

Although some themes are more likely to release strong feelings, this does depend very much on an individual's particular state at the time. The same theme can be light-hearted fun for one person and touch on something quite painful for another. Again, at the right time and in the right setting it can be therapeutic to look at painful issues; at the wrong time and place, or without adequate support, this can be experienced as a disaster.

Because of this variation of response, it is only possible to include with the themes very brief notes of any common difficulties. The task of choosing a suitable theme or activity and adapting it flexibly rests with the leader or therapist, who knows the group and the setting, and is aware of the atmosphere and issues on any particular occasion.

It is a good idea to re-read the section on 'Choosing an Activity or Theme' in Chapter 2 before embarking on the actual process of making a choice. Leaders and therapists working with particular client groups can also consult the notes in Chapter 6 on the suitability of themes for their group.

The activities and themes which follow may be regarded in the same way as tools, which may be used in many ways: constructively or destructively, clumsily or skilfully. Following this analogy, one needs to know before starting what tools can do, but expertise comes with the actual experience of using them.

Classification of Themes, Games and Exercises

This collection is divided into theme-centred sections, each with a brief introduction. These sections start with warm-up activities, exploring media, simple activities and general themes (B to E). Then comes a focus on the person, followed by a move outwards through relationships in families, pairs and groups (F to J). Finally, the links outward to other modes of expression are explored briefly (K to L). With the exception of the warm-up activities (which are numbered separately), the themes and activities are numbered continuously for easy reference.

Unless otherwise mentioned, most themes can be used with any two-dimensional medium, although obviously the medium chosen will affect what happens. Many can be adapted for use with less usual media such as clay, collage, etc. A Media Cross-reference (Section M) gives a few indications of some that have been tried. Section N provides a few notes on different media and their possibilities.

The collection was compiled chiefly from interviews with 40 art therapists in 1979, towards an MA dissertation at Birmingham Polytechnic. Existing collections in books and articles were also consulted; these are listed in the Bibliography. The collection was revised and additions made at the time of writing the material in the first half of the book.

A collection such as this can never be complete, for each theme can be adapted, changed or added to, so that it becomes a new one. Nor does it prescribe what to do: browsing through it may spark off an entirely different idea which is not included at all. It is up to everyone who uses this book to add their own ideas and develop this collection in whatever way they want.

A Checklist of Games, Themes and Exercises

C. MEDIA EXPLORATION

1. Doodles
2. Drawing Completions
3. Scribbles
4. Animal Marks
5. Colour Exploration
6. Linked Ideas
7. Opposing Modes
8. Contrasting Colours, Lines and Shapes
9. Shapes and Paint
10. Patterns
11. Using Mirrors
12. Choice of Media
13. Large-scale Work
14. Using Parts of the Body
15. Left Hand
16. Left and Right Hands
17. Eyes Closed
18. Creativity Mobilisation Technique
19. Wet Paper Techniques
20. Ink Blots and Butterflies
21. Prints and Rubbings
22. Mono-prints
23. Working from Observation
24. Five Senses
25. Clothes Line
26. Just Paper
27. Tissue Paper
28. Collage
29. Scratch the Surface
30. Wax-resist Pictures
31. Textures
32. Using 'Found Objects'
33. Junk Sculptures
34. Mixed Materials
35. Work with Clay
36. Sand Play
37. Letting off Steam
38. Papier-mâché
39. Play Dough
40. Creative Play with Food
41. Other Techniques

D. CONCENTRATION, DEXTERITY AND MEMORY

42. Planning a Garden
43. Domestic Animals Mural
44. Shelves
45. Shops and Categories
46. Breakfast Table
47. Daily Details
48. Clothes
49. Houses
50. National Flags
51. Map-making
52. Imaginary Traffic System
53. Objects
54. Fruit, Flowers and Leaves
55. Environments
56. Flower Collages
57. Experiences
58. Four Seasons
59. Natural Objects
60. Windows
61. Templates
62. Stencils
63. Initials Design
64. Circle Patterns
65. Patchwork Pattern Quilt
66. Weaving Patterns
67. Faces
68. Cut-out Shapes
69. Gifts

E. GENERAL THEMES

70. 'Four Elements' Picture Series
71. House — Tree — Person
72. Free Painting
73. Discussion Topic
74. Festival Themes

75. Themes of Life
76. Colour Associations
77. Subjects to Illustrate
78. Action and Conflict Themes
79. Personal Experiences

F. SELF-PERCEPTIONS

80. Introductions
81. Self-portraits: Realistic
82. Self-portraits: Images
83. Self-portraits Using Boxes
    and Bags
84. Life-size Self-portraits
85. 3-D Self-portraits
86. Masks
87. Names
88. Badges and Symbols
89. Metaphorical Portraits
90. Advertisements
91. Lifelines
92. Snakes and Ladders
93. Past, Present and Future
94. Life Collage
95. Life Priorities Collage
96. Aspects of Self
97. Recent Events
98. Childhood Memories
99. Life Review
100. Losses
101. Secrets and Privacy
102. Public and Private Masks
103. Good and Bad

104. Conflicts
105. Problems
106. Emotions
107. Present Mood
108. Objects and Feelings
109. Survival Needs
110. Wishes
111. Fears
112. Pictorial Narratives
113. Likes and Dislikes
114. Friendship Series
115. Perceptions of Self and
     One Other
116. Shadow of Self
117. Anima/Animus
118. Introvert/Extrovert
119. Personal Space
120. Personal Landscape
121. Personal Progression
122. Time Progression
123. Before and After Masks
124. Mask Diary
125. Reviewing Art Work
126. Institutions

G. FAMILY RELATIONSHIPS

Perceptions of Family

127. Family Portraits
128. Kinetic Family Drawings

129. Family Sculpture of
     Relationships

130. Inheritance
131. Family Comparisons
132. Childhood Memories
133. Re-enacting Parental
     Relationships

134. Family Themes
135. Family Relationships
     Through Play

Families in Action

136. Realistic Family Portraits
137. Abstract Family or Marital
     Relationship
138. Emotional Portraits
139. Present Situation
140. Important Things
141. Shared Experience
142. Problems and Problem-solving
143. Anger
144. Parents and Children

145. Boss-Slave
146. Single-parent Families
147. Grandparents' Influence
148. Family Sculpture in Action
149. Family Drawing or Painting
150. Sharing Resources
151. Teams
152. Art Evaluation Session
153. Other Pair or Group
     Activities

H. WORKING IN PAIRS

154. Drawing and Painting in Pairs
155. Conversations
156. Painting with an Observer
157. Sharing Space
158. Joint Pictures
159. Winnicott Squiggles
160. Introduction Interviews
161. Dialogue
162. Sequential Drawings

163. Portraits
164. First Impressions
165. Masks
166. Face Painting
167. Silhouettes
168. Relationships
169. Joint Project
170. Boss-Slave

I. GROUP PAINTINGS

171. Group Painting with Minimal
     Instructions
172. Co-operative Painting
173. Wall Newspaper
174. A Cohesive Whole
175. Moving On
176. Picking Out Images
177. Own Territories
178. Group 'Mandala'
179. Individual Starting Points

180. Group Stories
181. Fairy Story in Time Sequence
182. One-word-at-a-time Story
183. One-at-a-time Group
     Drawing
184. Group Murals on Themes
185. Solidarity
186. Building Islands and Worlds
187. Group Collage
188. Feelings Collage

189. Contributions
190. Moving Closer
191. Group Sculptures
192. Overlapping
    Group Transparency

193. Group Roles
194. Role-playing
195. Painting to Music
196. Individual Response to
    Group Painting

J. GROUP GAMES

197. Portraits
198. Portraits by Combined Effort
199. Badges and Totems
200. Group Symbol
201. Masks
202. Gifts
203. Shared Feelings
204. Metaphorical Portraits:
    Individuals
205. Metaphorical Portrait:
    Group
206. Interpretations
207. Interpretations in Action
208. Conflict Cartoons
209. Butterflies
210. Life-size Individuals and Group
211. Round Robin Drawings

212. Fill in the Gap
213. Leader Draws
214. Beautiful and Ugly
215. Secrets
216. Pool of Drawings
217. Group Additions
218. Group Sequential Drawing
219. Animal Consequences
220. Conversations in Paint
221. Situation Diagrams
222. Sociograms
223. Brainstorming Flow Diagram
224. Visual Whispers
225. Newspaper Games
226. Using Magazine Pictures
227. Trading Skills
228. Art Arena Games

K. GUIDED IMAGERY, DREAMS AND MEDITATIONS

Preparation for Visualisations

(a) Suitability
(b) Different Levels of Experience
(c) Levels of Relaxation
(d) The Journey or Visualisation

(e) Coming Back
(f) Painting
(g) Support
(h) Further Reading

Imaginative Journeys

229. Magic Carpet Ride
230. Wiseperson Guide
231. Gifts
232. Secret Garden and House
233. Secret Cave
234. Doorway

235. Mountain View
236. Magic Shop
237. Boat Journey
238. Shipwrecked on an Island
239. Five Senses

Identifications

240. Rosebush
241. Natural Objects
242. Dialogues

243. Moving Objects
244. River
245. Mythical Character

Other Ways of Stimulating Imagery

246. Group Fantasy
247. Listening to Music

248. Breathing in Light

Dreams, Myths, and Fairy Tales

249. Working with Dreams
250. Daydreams and Fantasies
251. Clay Monsters

252. Stories and Strip Cartoons
253. Myths
254. Fairy Tales

Painting as Meditation

255. Meditative Drawing and Painting
256. Mandala Possibilities

257. Autogenic Training
258. Colour Meditations

L. LINKS WITH OTHER EXPRESSIVE ARTS

Movement

259. Trust Walks
260. Emotions
261. Gesture Drawings

262. Acting Sensations
263. Dance

Drama

264. Sculpting Situations
265. Dialogues
266. Action and Conflict Themes
267. Accidents
268. Pictures Come to Life
269. Masks

270. Hats
271. Drama Games
272. Puppet Theatre
273. Theatrical Costumes
274. Story-telling and Plays
275. Tape Recorder

Poetry

276. Poetry as Stimulus
277. Poetry as Response

278. Concrete Poetry

Sound and Music

279. Sounds into Paint
280. Name Sounds

281. Moulding Sounds
282. Painting to Music

Multi-media

283. Letters
284. Evocative Adjectives
285. Stimulus to Paint
286. Response to Paint

287. Sensory Awareness
288. Music and Movement
289. Series of Sessions
290. Multi-media Events

B *Warm-up Activities*

Many leaders and therapists like to start group sessions with some kind of warm up, to get people going. This can be a physical/verbal activity or a simple painting activity. The first will help people to get into contact with each other, and the second will help people over the feelings of not knowing how to start to paint.

Physical/Verbal Activities

The Bibliography contains several collections for those who want to develop these. Here are some examples, very briefly described:

1. Name Games

(a) Claps alternate with names round the circle until names are familiar.
(b) First person says name, next person both names, third person all three names, and so on.
(c) Throw a bean-bag or other object from one person to another, catcher calls out name of thrower.

2. Quick Autobiographies

In pairs tell your partner about yourself for two minutes (or five minutes) and swap. Then partner introduces you to another pair or to whole group.

3. Paired Shares

In pairs, each person has three minutes' uninterrupted time to talk about anything she/he likes. Other person listens with full attention.

4. Rounds

These are quick ways of sharing personal information and getting people started. Everyone in turn says a few words or a sentence beginning:
On the way here I noticed ...
A good thing that happened this week was ...

114

Something I am excited about is ...
What I want from this group is ...
Right now I am feeling ...
etc.

5. *Handshakes*

Shake hands and introduce yourself to as many people as possible in the group.

6. *Mime Introductions*

People introduce themselves by each miming a characteristic activity or way of being.

7. *Mill and Grab*

Mill about, then leader calls 'Groups of three', and everyone gets into groups of three. Repeat for different size groups.

8. *Group and Regroup*

Leader calls different ways of grouping, e.g. all those with brown/blue eyes; all those wearing shoes with buckles/laces/neither, etc.

9. *Touch Colours*

Leader calls 'Everyone touch red' and everyone touches something red on their own or others' clothes. Repeat for other colours, and other qualities.

10. *Body Slaps*

Everyone slaps themselves all over, just hard enough to make themselves tingle.

11. *Back Slaps*

In a circle, everyone slaps the person in front's back (or all the way down). Then reverse circle and repeat with person on other side.

12. *Shoulder Massage*

In a circle, everyone massages the shoulders of the person in front. Then repeat with person on other side. This one follows on naturally from Back Slaps.

13. *Backboard*

People sit on floor in a circle, facing the next person's back. First person passes a short word on, by 'writing' it (with a finger) in capital letters on next person's back. When it has gone round circle, compare with original.

14. Pass the Mask

In a circle, first person pulls a face, then with their hands 'passes' the mask to the next person, who puts it on (imitates it), develops it into a new mask, which is then passed on.

15. Mirroring

In pairs, one person mirrors the other's actions. Swap roles and repeat.

16. Pushover

In pairs, starting in the middle of the room, each partner tries to push the other all the way to the wall.

17. Tick

In pairs, each person tries to touch partner in the small of the back, while partner tries to avoid this happening.

18. Trust Exercises

Rocking, lifting, blind walks, feeling and identifying faces, etc. (for groups where people already know each other to some extent).

19. Back-to-back

In pairs, sit back to back on the floor with knees bent. Link arms and try to stand up together.

20. Lap Circle

Needs at least a dozen people. Form a tight circle, all facing the same way, then everyone sits down on the lap behind at the same time.

21. Tangle

Hold hands in a line, then end person weaves under and round others until the whole group ends up in a tight tangle.

22. Knots

Stand in a circle with eyes closed, and each person clasps two other hands. Then open eyes, and without letting go of any hands, try to unravel the knot.

23. Simon Says

Leader issues instructions, which are only to be followed if prefaced by 'Simon says'. Anyone who gets it wrong is out.

24. Birthdays

In silence, using mime or gesture, get into a line in order of birthdays throughout the year.

25. Breathing

Sit with eyes closed, breathe deeply and rhythmically, drawing air right down, listening to breathing.

26. Dynamic Breathing

Keep repeating the sound 'who' while hopping from one leg to the other.

27. Movement Exercises

Simple movements such as shaking arms and legs, head rolls, stretching, awareness of limbs, relaxing, etc.

28. Limb Wiggles

Wiggle first one thumb, then the other, add fingers, arms, legs, bodies. Can also add moving round room and humming a tune, all at the same time!

29. Circle Dances

These are dances performed in one large circle, and usually have very simple movements. A music tape is needed, and someone who knows the basic steps of a few circle dances.

30. Preparation for Theme

Physical movement connected with theme, e.g. arm loosening exercises to introduce scribbles, spiral arm movements to introduce spiral lifeline, rhythm gestures to introduce movement to music followed by painting, etc.

Painting and Drawing Warm-ups

Several of the activities in Section C (Media Exploration) are good for helping people to make their first marks on paper in a non-threatening way. Some of the themes from Section F (Self-perceptions) also provide good starting points. Below are a few suggestions from these sections, together with one or two of the simpler ones from other sections:

C. Media Exploration

1. Doodles	10. Patterns
2. Drawing Completions	15. Left Hand
3. Scribbles	16. Left and Right Hands
4. Animal Masks	17. Eyes Closed
5. Colour Exploration	19. Wet Paper Techniques
8. Contrasting Colours, Lines and Shapes	20. Ink Blots and Butterflies
	27. Tissue Paper

D. Concentration, Dexterity and Memory

55. Environments
63. Initials Design

65. Patchwork Pattern Quilt
67. Faces

E. General Themes

71. House — Tree — Person

72. Free Painting

F. Self-perceptions

80. Introductions
87. Names
89. Metaphorical Portraits

97. Recent Events
107. Present Mood

H. Working in Pairs

158(f). Joint Pictures
159. Winnicott Squiggles

160. Introduction Interviews
161. Dialogue

I. Group Paintings

183(e), (k). Pass Around Paper/Clay
183(h). Introductions

195(a), (b). Movement to Music,
followed by Painting

J. Group Games

211. Round Robin Drawings
212. Fill in the Gap

219. Animal Consequences

C Media Exploration

The ideas in this section concentrate on different ways of exploring media, to develop imagination and creativity. Some of the suggestions overlap with or lead into themes listed in other sections. Many of them offer ways into using art materials, and stimulate the playfulness needed to be spontaneous. They can be useful for new groups, or for people who are worried about making their first mark on a piece of paper.

1. Doodles

There are many ways of doodling, but the essence is to let a pen or crayon wander aimlessly, or 'go for a walk with a line', until something meaningful emerges. This is then worked on. Some variations:

(a) Keep a 'doodle diary' and see if doodles change over a period of time.
(b) Close eyes to doodle, let the crayon draw as it wants. Open eyes, find image and develop.
(c) Use lines, colours and sounds without feeling there 'should' be an end-product. Let a colour 'pick you'.
(d) From a number of doodles, select the ones liked best and least.
(e) Evolve a story from a spontaneous doodle.
(f) Verbalise feelings as doodle and something emerges.
(g) Winnicott squiggle in pairs — see No. 159.
(h) Metamorphosis: change picture in three moves to something else.
(i) Use dirty marks on paper as basis for associations to develop an image.
(j) Group can use marks on dirty wall as in (i).
(k) See also No. 20.
(l) Draw own initials as large as possible, and use to find picture or design to develop. This can be less threatening than scribbles because the initials are already familiar.

2. Drawing Completions

From a given starting point of simple lines and shapes, complete a picture. The different results from different members of the group can provoke

119

lively discussion. There can be visual (e.g. thickness of line) as well as symbolic differences.

Variations:

(a) Start with a circle, make it represent something, then add something inside, outside or on the line.

(b) See also No. 20.

3. Scribbles

Use whole body to make scribbles with large movements, possibly with eyes closed. Looking from all sides, find forms that suggest a picture and develop it.

4. Animal Marks

Imagine that your paintbrush is an insect (e.g. a grasshopper) and make marks on the paper. Then imagine it is a snake and make marks as if it were sliding across the paper, and so on for other creatures.

5. Colour Exploration

Using one colour only, and white paper, explore the meaning of this colour for you, e.g. by drawing shapes and lines in that colour.

Variations:

(a) Select colour(s) most liked or disliked.

(b) Select two or three colours to represent a harmonious group, or express strands of personality, or show moods.

(c) Select colours to counterbalance negative moods.

(d) Start with one colour, then mix in another.

(e) Paint with two or three colours on large paper.

(f) Select a colour liked and a colour disliked, and make some kind of painting. Can go on to using two colours disliked.

(g) Do two paintings with colours most liked/disliked, and compare.

(h) Starting with one colour, perhaps in connection with a theme (e.g. seasons), move to another, making a 'mosaic carpet' of colours. See if this gives rise to any particular image.

(i) Choose a large paintbrush and a colour, close your eyes and try to cover the paper with marks. Open your eyes and look. Then choose another colour.

(j) Coloured backgrounds: do a series of paintings on different coloured papers. Before starting, make associations with each colour of paper, and use these to develop the paintings.

6. Linked Ideas

Work on a series of linked ideas or felt experiences by starting a new piece of work before the previous piece is finished. This can eliminate the fear of starting, and promote a flow of ideas.

7. Opposing Modes

Begin painting in any way that comes naturally, then deliberately alter your approach, and notice the effect. Repeat frequently while allowing notions of form to arise and be developed.

Variation: Work quickly on a painting, then if there is a pattern, experiment with the opposite of what you usually do.

8. Contrasting Colours, Lines and Shapes

Use colours, lines, shapes, curves, etc. to create contrasts, e.g. light and heavy strokes, long and short, light and dark, bright and dull, etc.

Variation: After working with contrasts separately, work on ways of bringing them together.

9. Shapes and Paint

Draw any shape you like, cut it out and add to it by drawing and painting. Repeat with a different shape.

Variation: Stick shape on a background and add to it in the same way.

10. Patterns

Good ways of getting going. Some pattern suggestions:

(a) Repeated shapes. Choose three colours and a simple line form such as a rectangle, arc, etc. Use this shape in different ways, different colours, orientations, sizes, overlaps. If a pattern emerges, develop it with shading and connections.

(b) Repeat (a) using opposite kind of shape in opposite kind of way.

(c) Squares and circles; op art.

(d) Draw ten bubbles and take line round bubbles; fill in with colours.

(e) Take line for a walk — dashes, zigzags, bubbles.

(f) Make a simple shape and repeat it, changing a little each time. Form several of them into a pattern. Try using one colour first, then adding other colours.

(g) Tear out shapes and look at the patterns they can make. Then look at the spaces between the shapes and make a further pattern from these.

(h) Start with a thick wavy line, then draw thin lines on either side, altering the shape as you go. See if it suggests anything.

(i) Tissue paper patterns — see No. 27.

(j) Make 3-D patterns using paper, toilet roll centres, matchboxes or other junk materials.

(k) Make textured patterns using collage materials or dabs of paint.

(l) Arrange cut-out shapes in a pattern, which can be altered from day to day.

11. Using Mirrors

Use wax crayons in three colours to do an abstract pattern in soft textures.

Then look at the images formed by placing in corner of two mirrors at right-angles to each other.
Variation: Group of four people produces pattern of soft textures, using one colour each, working in silence; use mirrors as above.

12. Choice of Media

Complete a given project in a single medium or mixed media. The project can be a set theme, or left open. Reflect on the choices made.

13. Large-scale work

Large-scale work using rollers, decorating brushes, sponges, rags, feet, hands, etc. Often best done outside in fine weather!
Variations:
(a) Individual free expression on large sheet of paper.
(b) Roll liquid paint on to large card, then use shakers to shake powder colour on.
(c) Use variety of rolling objects to trail liquid paint from paint trays over long piece of paper.

14. Using Parts of the Body

Use various parts of the body to paint, e.g. fingerpainting, using palms and feet to make prints, etc.
Variations:
(a) Use toes, heels, etc. to increase awareness of feet.
(b) See Nos. 15 and 16.

15. Left Hand

Try painting with opposite hand from usual one. This is good for loosening up.
Variations:
(a) With a large paintbrush and one colour, make marks on paper. Change colour and repeat.
(b) Fingerpaint with opposite hand from usual one.
(c) Undertake any theme with opposite hand from usual one.

16. Left and Right Hands

Let your right hand choose a colour for itself, and the left the same. Experiment with colours, eyes closed. Open eyes and draw with both hands and both colours. Share experiences in the group.
Variations: Draw or copy a picture, first with usual hand and then with opposite one.

17. Eyes Closed

Draw or paint with your eyes closed. Good for those worried about being

unable to control their drawing, or who are product-oriented, as perfection is recognisably impossible.
Variations:
(a) Left and right hands, see No. 16,
(b) Colour exploration, see No. 5(i).

18. *Creativity Mobilisation Technique*

This is a non-verbal technique developed by Wolfgang Luthe to mobilise the brain functions to increased creativity. Detailed instructions are contained in his book *Creativity Mobilisation Technique* (Grune and Stratton, New York, 1976). Here is a very brief summary:
(a) cover 70 to 90 per cent of a double sheet of newspaper in two minutes so that it makes the biggest possible mess.
(b) Make a series of 15 such 'no thought' mess paintings.
(c) Engage in at least one painting session on four different days a week.
(d) Continue regular painting sessions for at least four to six weeks.
(e) Keep a diary of each session.

19. *Wet Paper Techniques*

Wet the paper and use wet paint, brushed, splattered or poured on. Watch the colours merge, and notice feelings involved.
Variations:
(a) Crumple the paper as well as wetting it.
(b) Develop resulting shapes into an image.
(c) Use felt pens to draw around and between the blotches.
(d) Give titles to several quickly done 'blotches'.

20. *Ink Blots and Butterflies*

Drop ink or thick blobs of paint on paper, fold in half, then unfold. Develop any image that is suggested.
Variations:
(a) Give similar ink blots to different members of the group to develop, and compare results.
(b) See also Nos. 1 and 2.
(c) Cut out and mount a part of the blob that is particularly liked (this can help to regain a feeling of control over the process).

21. *Prints and Rubbings*

Use junk materials and textured objects to dip in paint and make prints; or place underneath paper and make rubbings.
Variations:
(a) Use outside objects in fine weather.
(b) Group pictures of different rubbings and textures.
(c) Use prints to make a pattern.

22. Mono-prints

Spread paint of a creamy consistency (e.g. powder paint) on a smooth surface such as stone, glass or melamine. Make a pattern or picture in the paint, with fingers, back of a paintbrush or other instrument. Press paper on top to make a print, and then remove. Add more paint if necessary and repeat the process. This is useful for children (or adults) whose attempts to express ideas are frustrated by their lack of drawing ability.

Variation: Use printing ink and a roller to roll it on to glass.

23. Working from Observation

Bring in things to draw from observation, then make a group picture from these, e.g. leaves, fruit, hands, tools, faces, etc.

Variations:

(a) From observation, move on to questions about feelings concerned with objects.

(b) Study a flower intensely and then paint it.

24. Five Senses

Think about what colour you would associate with the present month. Then see what each of the five senses would suggest for that month. Try to relate all these aspects to yourself in a picture or poem. Particularly good for winter months when things are apparently lifeless.

25. Clothes Line

Paint on sheets of paper pegged to a clothes line. Compare this with painting on a sheet of paper on a table.

26. Just Paper

Each person in the group has one sheet of paper to use in some way to represent personal time, for 20 minutes. The paper can be torn, sellotaped, chewed, etc., but not drawn on. The process can be reflected on by describing it; describing the product if any; noting any personal association.

Variations:

(a) Pass a piece of paper around the group, doing anything you like to it in silence, until the paper has disintegrated.

(b) Each person makes something quickly from one sheet of paper, glue and scissors.

(c) Group makes construction from rolls of newspaper, e.g. jungle and occupants.

(d) Use three pieces of paper (and glue) to
    (i) get a message from the desert to someone that you're okay;
    (ii) make a present for the group;
    (iii) make a representation of the institution.

(e) (Good for children) Fold and cut paper dolls, animals and other figures, evolving stories about animal families, zoos, etc. as you proceed.

27. Tissue Paper

Tear up different colours of tissue paper and paste on a sheet of white paper to make abstract design. Good for people who feel they cannot draw or paint.
Variations:
(a) Use only one colour of tissue paper.
(b) Cut tissue paper instead of tearing.
(c) Tissue paper work on windows.
(d) Build up tissue paper faces on paper plates.
(e) Tissue paper and wire sculptures.

28. Collage

There are many ways of experimenting with collage materials and magazine pictures, e.g:
(a) Patchwork pattern quilt, see No. 65.
(b) Cut out and stick pictures of people, and write down what they might be thinking or saying.
(c) Stick pieces of different fabrics on paper, then colour in between to create abstract design.
(d) Cut out pictures of landscapes and write down any associations.

29. Scratch the Surface

Cover a whole paper with colours using felt-tips or pencils. Then cover this with a layer of dark wax crayon or oil pastel. Scratch a design in the surface so that underlying colours show through.

30. Wax-resist Pictures

Draw patterns or pictures with the end of a candle (or a wax crayon) on fairly absorbent paper, then cover the paper with watery paint to make the picture appear.

31. Textures

Collect a variety of objects with different textures, and after feeling them (preferably with eyes closed), paint a response to them or try to represent the texture in paint. This can be done in pairs or in a group.
Variation: Create a mini-environment from textured materials that describe your personality, forming a 'touch box'.

32. Using 'Found Objects'

Collect natural and artificial objects, preferably from your own environ-

ment, e.g. shells, flowers, ornaments, leaves, plants, rocks, stones, sand, water, sawdust, etc., and create a picture, collage, structure, etc. This can be on a specified theme, or left open.
Variations:
(a) Outline bodies on huge piece of paper, and fill in with collage of variously textured materials (see No. 84(c)).
(b) Collage from different kinds of crackers or pasta.

33. Junk Sculptures

Similar to No. 32, but using piles of assorted rubbish. There are many different ways of using rubbish, e.g.
(a) Make puppets (this can be extended to plays, puppet shows and acting).
(b) Group sculpture from scrap wood, newspaper rolls or other materials.
(c) Landscape on large board.
(d) Mobiles.
(e) Work with semi-precious junk, e.g. pearls, glitter, etc.
(f) Make a particular object.

34. Mixed Materials

Divide into small groups. Each small group is given an envelope of mixed materials (e.g. large paper, tissue paper, coloured sticky squares, drinking straws, paper strengtheners, coloured sellotape, etc.) to make a picture or object connected with a particular theme, e.g. transport. Good for mixed groups of adults and children.

35. Work with Clay

There are very many ways of working with clay, e.g:
(a) Getting to know it as a material — feeling, pressing, squeezing, shaping, etc; using all the senses to experience it.
(b) Make ball of clay into something with eyes closed.
(c) Describe clay creation in first person.
(d) Making impressions on clay with other implements.
(e) Specified theme, e.g. individual houses for group street scene.
(f) Making simple slab pots and thumb pots.
(g) Using glazes.

36. Sand Play

Use sandbox and miniature figures of animals and people to portray situations and tell stories. Useful for children and others with communication difficulties; can be used to relive life conflicts in imaginative play.

37. Letting Off Steam

This can be encouraged with certain materials, if freely available, e.g:

(a) Smashing up wood offcuts, banging nails.
(b) Large-scale work, see No. 13.
(c) Junk sculptures, see No. 33.
(d) Clay work, thumping and wedging it.
(e) Creativity mobilisation technique, see No. 18.
(f) Newspaper sculpture involving tearing and sticking, see No. 26(c).
(g) Paper techniques, see No. 26(a).
(h) Sand play, see No. 36.

38. Papier-mâché

Make up about half a packet of Polycell or similar paste in a bucket, and fill with strips of torn (not cut) newspaper to soak. Use moulds to make models (first grease with Vaseline). Allow a few days for papier-mâché to dry, then paint. Particularly useful for:
(a) Masks, modelled over plasticine or clay, or over a balloon (which is then 'popped').
(b) Puppets.
(c) Models of all kinds.

39. Play Dough

There are several recipes. Here are two slightly different ones:
(a) Mix 2 cups plain flour, $^3/_4$ cup salt, 1tbsp. oil, $^1/_2$ cup water to consistency of pastry. The amount of water may need to be varied according to flour. Food colouring or powder paint can be added.
(b) Boil 1tbsp. oil and 4 (or more) tbsp. water. Add this to 1 cup plain flour, 2tbsp. salt, 2tsp. cream of tartar and food colouring or powder paint. (The heat helps to bind the dough and the cream of tartar helps the play dough to keep longer and gives it a smoother feel.)
Keep in plastic bag or box in refrigerator. Can be made into play food or used as modelling material. Especially useful for young children.

40. Creative Play with Food

Make or decorate biscuits with faces and work out dialogues before eating them up!
Variation: Use other kinds of food connected together with toothpicks or cocktail sticks.

41. Other Techniques

There is a great variety of materials and techniques which can be used in a creative way to stimulate the imagination. Here are some:
(a) Plaster of Paris, e.g. landscape, sand castings, sculptures, carvings. The plaster can be poured into an old carton to set, and the box then removed, to give a lump for carving; or it can be spread on chicken-wire to make larger structures. Plaster sets very quickly and Polyfilla

can sometimes be used if slower setting is desired. Plaster-impregnated bandages are quick and easy to use.

(b) Silk-screen printing, e.g. designs made from newspapers.

(c) Butterfly paintings and potato printing — see also Nos. 20 and 21.

(d) Scratchboard pictures.

(e) Marbling.

(f) Abstract sculpture from wood offcuts and other materials.

(g) Batik and fabric-printing.

(h) Tie-and-dye T-shirts and materials.

(i) Candle-making.

(j) Lino cuts.

(k) Pin-and-thread pictures.

(l) Kite-making.

(m) Balloon masks from papier mâché over balloons, see No. 38.

(n) Blowing paint through straws.

(o) Mosaics.

(p) Making stencils.

(q) String prints: dip string in paint, place on paper, fold paper and withdraw string while pressing down paper.

D *Concentration, Dexterity and Memory*

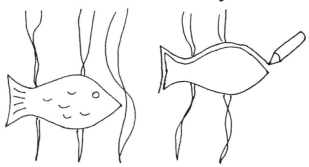

Many of these activities try to increase or maintain skills of concentration, dexterity and memory. They can be useful learning activities for children and mentally handicapped people, and for long-term patients being rehabilitated to leave an institution after many years. Some of them are also useful for elderly people with senility problems, in helping them to retain their hold on 'reality' (especially if they have to live in an institution). Even more important, they can use experiences people may have had during their lives, and reaffirm their personal value in remembering what they have done.

42. *Planning a Garden*

Useful for those who have done a lot of gardening. Plan a garden, using drawing, painting and collage, etc.

43. *Domestic Animals Mural*

Using prepared templates, everyone draws his or her own version, paints and cuts out. These can then be fitted into prepared spaces on a mural, and the background painted in.

44. *Shelves*

Using prepared paper with shelves drawn on it, imagine it as a larder and decide what to stock it with.
Variations:
(a) Garden shed.
(b) Tool cupboard.
(c) Table top — what sort of meal?
(d) Washing line — what is hanging out?
(e) Shop window — what is in it?

45. *Shops and Categories*

Provide each member of the group with a sheet of blank paper with a different shop heading, e.g. shoe shop, grocer, garage, baker, etc. Then 'stock' the shops with appropriate articles, either drawn or cut from magazines.

Variations:

(a) Head each sheet with a different colour and stick on articles of the correct colour.

(b) Each sheet headed sport, cookery and other activities.

(c) Other categories, e.g. furniture, clothes, etc.

46. Breakfast Table

Table is covered with a sheet of paper and real things — such as a teapot, toast, etc. Imagine a fantasy meal — draw what you would like to have for breakfast on paper, using the real objects to draw around or copy if needed. Group works all around the table.

Variation: Use cardboard cut-outs if real things not available.

47. Daily Details

Draw or cut out pictures of daily life, e.g. recent meals, events, people, clothes, etc., remembering and talking about details in the process.

48. Clothes

Photocopy a magazine portrait high up on a piece of paper. Draw rest of person in any clothes you wish.

Variation: Draw own clothing from memory.

49. Houses

Supply outlines of a house for people to fill in with whatever details they want, and add further items and figures if desired. (This may lead to discussion of families and people at home.)

50. National Flags

Have available copies of various national flags to colour in. Members of the group choose the ones they want and may make associations with them. (Good for groups of elderly people who may have visited other countries, e.g. in wartime.)

51. Map-making

Draw bus, ambulance, walking or cycling routes to school, club, hospital, day centre, etc., or to any other place of interest.

52. Imaginary Traffic System

Using a collection of miniature cars, draw a large road system of a town, putting in other buildings, etc.

53. Objects

Divide a sheet of paper into, say, eight boxes, each with a different heading, e.g. a bird, a chair, a car, an animal. Group members then draw or stick an appropriate picture in each box.

54. Fruit, Flowers and Leaves

Draw or trace around leaves, flowers, fruit, found objects, etc. Paint and cut out. Make into collage as a group.
Variation: Combined murals of butterflies, fish, sunflowers, etc.

55. Environments

Cut out a magazine figure, and then fill in environment around it.

56. Flower Collages

Make individual flower collages in polystyrene dishes. Display collages as a group.
Variation: Use other themes for individual panels, see No. 189(a).

57. Experiences

Discuss experiences of, e.g. seeing a rainbow; then try to capture memory of this by painting rainbow, trees, hills, clouds, rain, etc. Can be applied to any experience likely to be common to the group, e.g. a recent outing.

58. Four Seasons

Take four differently coloured large sheets of paper and ask the group to choose which colour will be for each of the four seasons. Then cut out magazine pictures and stick on appropriate sheet of paper.

59. Natural Objects

Use natural objects as stimulation for discussion, painting murals.

60. Windows

Adaptation of No. 120(a). Have a variety of 'windows'. Draw view through window and what is in room (looking in or out).

61. Templates

Provide templates, then the group uses them to draw around on card, cut out and stick on murals, e.g. festival themes, see No. 74.

62. Stencils

Similar to templates, but people draw inside the shape. Can also be used to apply paint to murals, and for making repeating patterns.

63. Initials Design

Write your initials and make a design out of it.
Variations:
(a) Use your name or nickname.
(b) Repeat each letter upside down and look at patterns and spaces made
    by shapes. Develop into a design.

64. Circle Patterns

Have prepared a large circle divided into segments like an orange. Group
starts at the middle and works outwards, producing patterns of colour,
shape, line, etc. (can also stick things on).
Variations: Use any other shape broken down into smaller shapes, see No.
189(b), (c), (d).

65. Patchwork Pattern Quilt

Cut out lots of 'patchwork' shapes from coloured paper and magazines.
Then group members create their own pattern of 'quilt' from the pieces.
Variation: Create a large 'quilt' by everyone working on the same pattern.

66. Weaving Patterns

Weave a pattern with coloured strips of paper, working out own pattern.

67. Faces

Using prepared circles, draw faces on circles.
Variations:
(a) If this is too difficult, make a stencil.
(b) Different kinds of faces: a funny face, a sad face, a silly face, etc.

68. Cut-out Shapes

Cut out shapes of people, men and women (or have them prepared), and
fill them in using any desired medium.
Variations:
(a) Butterfly shapes.
(b) Animal shapes.

69. Gifts

Make or draw something you would like to give to someone.

E *General Themes*

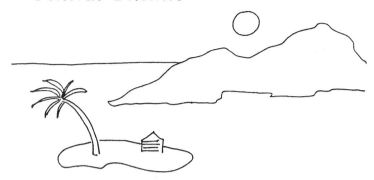

There are many themes which, although general rather than personal, can enable people to bring out important feelings in the process of painting and subsequent discussion.

70. 'Four Elements' Picture Series

This series based on the four ancient elements of air, earth, fire and water. Paint 24 pictures on the themes below, each on a separate sheet:
(a) Earth series: cave — hut — house — courtyard — field — earth.
(b) Water series: spring — brook — river — lake — sea — water.
(c) Air series: breath — wind — storm — cloud — sky/heaven — air.
(d) Fire series: torch — fireplace — lamp — hearth/fire — light — fire.
These can be used as discussion points, comparing pictures of same series and comparing how different people have interpreted the theme. Some people will find that they have more affinity to one series than others and this can be a basis for discussion.
Variation: Choose only one theme (earth, water, air or fire) and do a painting on any aspect of this theme.

71. House — Tree — Person

Draw a house, a tree and a person (or face). Or select one of these and set it for a group.
Variations:
(a) Add landscape.
(b) Describe each one in the first person.
(c) Paint your home, or an ideal house, or an ideal island.

72. Free Painting

Paint a picture in 15-20 minutes. Show it to the group and say as much as you want to say. No analysis. This gives people who are prepared to share their personal feelings the space and 'permission' to do so.

133

73. Discussion Topic

Use a theme which has arisen from group discussion as the theme of artwork, either individual or group.

74. Festival Themes

There are many possibilities for personal work or for groupwork which can use particular festivals as starting points, e.g:
(a) Exploring festival symbols.
(b) Celebration of festivals, e.g. spring, in group pictures.
(c) New Year resolutions.
(d) Mammoth birthday card for a member of the group.
(e) Easter theme.
(f) Practical projects such as decorations for Christmas, Valentine's Day, Hallowe'en.
(g) Posters for events or to get over ideas.
(h) The four seasons.
(i) Jumble sale — drawings of rubbish.
Even though most of these themes celebrate joyful events, they may also bring back memories of happier times. They may thus reinforce present feelings of isolation and depression, especially if people are in institutions. It is important to be aware of this.

75. Themes of Life

Choose a particular life theme and make a picture connected with it, e.g. sex, marriage, family; authority, freedom, growth, life and death; leaving, goodbye; the group, communication, problems; life, light, love; a force that affects your life strongly, etc. Topics may need some introduction to get started.

76. Colour Associations

Associate colours with abstract states, e.g:
(a) Emotions — sadness, fear, love, joy, calm, etc.
(b) Periods of your life — babyhood, childhood, etc.
(c) Seasons.
(d) Times of day.
(e) Psychic function — thinking, feeling, intuition, sensation, etc.
(f) Types of people — extrovert, introvert, etc.
(g) Members of your family, and other influential people.

77. Subjects to Illustrate

These can relate to personal experiences or provide a more covert way of expressing oneself. Children and adolescents can often use them in this way. There is an infinite number of such themes; here are a few:

(a) Nature — desert, mountain, rock, plants, trees, animals, birds, fish, shells.
(b) Weather — storm, thunder and lightning, sun, snow, rain, cloud, wind, fire, hot day, twilight, moonlight.
(c) Water — raindrops, waterfalls, whirlpools, ripples, waves, sea, river, lake, etc.
(d) Gardens — secret gardens, mazes, labyrinths.
(e) Changed perspectives — ant's — or bird's — or elephant's eye view.
(f) People — villain, devil, ghosts, magician, angel, witch, fairies, clown.
(g) Religious — nativity, God; good and evil; heaven and hell, etc.
(h) Dreams and nightmares (see also No. 249).
(i) Group situations — fight, war, circus, fair, orchestra, etc.
(j) Fantasy — other planets, outer space, exploring a cave, character from TV or story, etc.
(k) Events — the weekend, a day trip, my day, my week; journeys made, expected or desired, etc.

78. *Action and Conflict Themes*

These can be useful for those who cannot easily articulate their conflicts, but can depict them graphically through another situation; for instance, some children and adolescents.
(a) Graffiti on large sheets of paper.
(b) Ghosts and skeletons.
(c) Fires, e.g. ship on fire.
(d) Life on another planet.
(e) In prison (from inside or outside).
(f) 'Wanted' posters.
(g) Sport — boxing, football, etc.
(h) Storms, e.g. at sea; or stormy sky with sunny part in corner.
(i) Explosions, volcanoes, etc.
(j) Battles.
(k) Underwater pictures.
(l) Prehistoric or mythical monsters; monster inside someone's head; horrible slimy creature in mud; creating and despatching one's own monster.
(m) Murder.
(n) Moods, e.g. mood changes; sad and miserable; angry; happy thoughts; frightened; excited; peaceful; lonely; trapped; feeling ill.
(o) Draw around hands and wrists, then add watch, rings, scars, veins, tattoos, etc.

79. *Personal Experiences*

Art work around events people have experienced, e.g. a special trip, a particular ward, etc.

Variation for children: Experiences with pets and animals. This can evoke strong feelings of protectiveness, responsibility, fear or violence, according to the experience; it may be easier for some children to express their feelings about animals than about people.

F Self-perceptions

Most of this section is concerned, in a variety of ways, with how people see themselves. This can be a refreshing and reflective experience for many people, but can be too confrontative for very hurt or damaged people, who may find the less direct themes in Section E more suitable.

80. Introductions

The idea of this is to introduce yourself to the group on paper. This can be less threatening than a verbal introduction, as everyone does it at once. Additional instructions can include drawing whatever might describe yourself, including your name, etc.

Variations:
(a) Produce poster for display for duration of group/conference, etc.
(b) Poster to illustrate your lifestyle for another person.
(c) Include specific attitudes, interests, characteristics, family, friends, etc.
(d) Use collage.
(e) Bring to first meeting of group.
(f) Personal worlds: visualise your world in colours, lines, shapes and symbols, or how you would like it to be.

81. Self-portraits: Realistic

Do a realistic portrait of yourself, in pastels, paint or clay, making sure that details, etc. are right.

Variations:
(a) Self-portrait from memory — face or nude.
(b) Quick realistic portrait, in two minutes or other time limit.
(c) Clay self-portrait with eyes closed; touch face with one hand, modelling with the other.
(d) Touch face, then draw it.
(e) Draw nude figure of yourself. Then, at home, compare your drawing with what you see in mirror. (This exercise may be best done individually and then shared in the group.)
(f) Make movable clay and wire marionette to resemble self, with environ-

ment to scale. This helps to accept physical reality through transitional object.
(g) Select photograph most like oneself. Can be good for helping discussion of handicaps, e.g. mothers with handicapped children.

82. Self-portraits: Images

Do self-portrait:
(i) how you see yourself or feel inside yourself;
(ii) how others (e.g. someone close) see you (or how you present yourself).
They can be realistic or abstract.
Variations:
(a) Add a third contrast: how you would like to be seen.
(b) Use clay or collage; or mixed media.
(c) How you see yourself today/right now.
(d) Yourself as seen by sympathetic friend; and by someone you dislike.
(e) As for (d), but write about yourself from these two points of view.
(f) Only do 'How I perceive myself'.
(g) Imagine piece of paper is mirror on door — what do you see? (realistic, metaphorical or abstract).
(h) Four selves — actual, perceived, ideal, future.
(i) Self box — see No. 83.
(j) Self-portrait, exaggerating how you think you look.
(k) Apply to particular roles, e.g. professional self.
(l) Make several masks to show different aspects of yourself that you show in different circumstances, and also a mask to show how you really feel.
(m) As for (l), but show all the aspects on one mask.
(n) As for (l) or (m) but use collage materials or 'media images' cut from magazine.

83. Self-portraits Using Boxes and Bags

Use collage images to represent how you feel inside and outside yourself by using inside and outside of box, bag or other container.
Variations:
(a) Symbol of important goal on top of upturned box, and symbols of what you want to change on the sides of the box. (Acrylic paints, which dry very quickly, can be used to make further changes.)
(b) Outside of box showing your roles, inside of box filled with objects or pictures relating to your values, friends, family, hobbies, things important to you.
(c) Use junk materials.
(d) Use paper bags to paste pictures on outside of what you show to the world, and put inside what you keep inside.

(e) Repeat (d) above for others close to you, e.g. mother, father, spouse, children, etc. Are there similarities?

(f) Draw or paint abstract symbols on separate pieces of paper to represent your values. Put inside the bag those you always have, a˙ ¹ outside those which apply only to your present situation.

(g) Paste outside the best things that can happen to you. Inside put a collection of your fears.

Photograph 17 shows a group at an alcoholics unit sharing ideas on using junk materials to make self-portraits in tins and boxes.

84. Life-size Self-portraits

Pin a large roll of paper to the wall, draw round yourself, then work on the life-size body image in any way you like.

Variations:

(a) Person lies on floor and someone else traces round on paper.

(b) Life-size body image of how you use the different parts of your body to communicate how you feel.

(c) Trace body outline, name parts and fill in with colours or collage materials, or with what is going on inside you, physically and mentally; or with lines of energy.

(d) Draw silhouettes of body parts, cut out and arrange on a mural.

(e) Life-size portrait of what it is like to be yourself right now.

(f) Talk to your outline; imagine yourself in front of you.

(g) Choose a section of body image to explore in another painting.

(h) See if a parent is associated with any particular part of the body.

(i) (Good for children) Fill in with own likeness, e.g. hair and clothes worn.

(j) Make life-size model to act as 'other self'.

(k) Use full-length mirror (good for children).

85. 3-D Self-portraits

Build a representation of yourself in 3-D, using junk materials.

Variations:

(a) Self box (see No. 83). Or use junk materials inside and outside box.

(b) Work with large lump of clay in any way, without trying to make a model. When finished, place on table to reflect where you would feel comfortable if the clay were you.

(c) Make a movable clay marionette to resemble yourself.

(d) Make a relief clay portrait inside a shoebox; let it dry and paint it.

(e) Eyes closed, visualise a round ball changing into a realistic or abstract image of yourself. Then create image with hands. Open eyes to finish off.

(f) Clay hands: roll some clay into a ball and press down with one hand to make a 'handprint'. Scratch a symbol which represents something

17: Self-portraits in Boxes, Using Junk Materials — Alcoholics Unit

(Photograph by Paul Curtis)

friendly about you. Repeat for a hand of a person you like and arrange two hands in suitable positions.

(g) See also Nos. 81(c) and 82(b).

86. Masks

Make a mask of yourself. Put it on and act the role your mask suggests.
Variations:
(a) Make a mask to express a particular emotion — see also No. 106.
(b) Make up/use stories which involve masks.
(c) Link up with No. 82, masks of how you see yourself and how others see you.
(d) See also No. 103. Masks to represent ideal and unacceptable sides of yourself.
(e) See also Nos. 123 and 124 for other uses of masks.

87. Names

Draw images of:
(i)   your nickname when a child;
(ii) your proper name;
(iii) a fantasy name.
Variations:
(a) Pick a name for yourself according to your feelings and embellish it in some way.
(b) Using opposite hand from usual, write your name:
    (i)   backwards;
    (ii) forwards to fill the whole space;
    (iii) very slowly.
Combine with other exercises about yourself.

88. Badges and Symbols

Find and draw your own symbol. (If this is difficult, think of other everyday visual symbols first.)
Variations:
(a) Develop your own symbol for use on a personal shield.
(b) Make up a strip cartoon using your own symbol.
(c) Make a badge for yourself to represent a quality of yours that you are proud of.
(d) Make up a symbol for a personal T-shirt.
(e) Make up a slogan to go with your symbol.
(f) Make own coat of arms with motto, symbol, epitaph, etc.

89. Metaphorical Portraits

Draw yourself as some kind of object. The choice of object can be left open to see what is produced, or it can be specified, e.g. draw yourself as a house,

tree, animal, food, island, colours and shapes, building, flower, plant, meal, water, tree or landscape. If appropriate, include a setting.
Variations:
(a) After drawing the object, talk about it in the first person, act as if you were that object.
(b) What object (animal, building, etc.) would you like to be?
(c) What object (animal, building, etc.) would you be if reincarnated?
(d) Draw yourself as an object which represents how you are feeling today.
(e) Draw yourself as the animal (etc.) you would:
   (i)   most like to be;
   (ii) least like to be.
(f) Draw yourself as an object and as an animal, on opposite sides of the paper. (Do these relate to how you are treated by others, or how you relate to others?)
(g) Dynamic metaphors, e.g. using an image of a developing seed; illustrate a point of growth which relates to you, noting reactions to process of growth.
(h) Choose several colours and make a drawing that represents yourself.
(i) For people who tend to isolate themselves, ask for a setting to be included.

90. Advertisements

Draw/paint an advertisement for yourself. This can involve 'selling oneself' and bring up negative feelings from lack of self-esteem, and can also involve thinking about the sort of people to be attracted by the advertisement.
Variations:
(a) After each person has finished, others in the group add to each advertisement aspects missed out.
(b) Advertisement to sell you as a friend, worker, parent, etc.
(c) Write or draw advertisements for others.
(d) Depict a department store displaying your personal qualities. After this, a 'shopping trip' to select wares from others' stores to make another picture.

91. Lifeline

Draw your life as a line, journey or road-map. Put in images and events along the way, drawn and/or written.
Variations:
(a) Select one section of your line and draw an image.
(b) Choose one part only to depict as a line, or a particular aspect, e.g. friends, work life, sexual life, etc.
(c) Use sections labelled 'past', 'present' and 'future'.

(d) Draw your life as a maze, if appropriate.
(e) Use the whole piece of paper to depict your lifetime, or use a roll of paper.
(f) Lifeline as a spiral, starting from birth.
(g) Continue lifeline into future.
(h) Illustrate your life story with images from magazines.
(i) Draw map of important things, places and people in your life.
(j) Place special emphasis on where you are going.
(k) Survey past art work from specific period.
(l) Include barriers and detours, and role play passing these.
(m) Story of how you came to particular situation, e.g. prison, hospital, in trouble, etc.

92. *Snakes and Ladders*

Devise your own game of snakes and ladders, using events and images from your life as 'snakes' and 'ladders'. Play your game with another person.

93. *Past, Present and Future*

This is another view of the same theme as No. 91, but in more distinct blocks. Draw images of your past, present and hoped-for future.
Variations:
(a) Concentrate on future only.
(b) Use images from magazine.
(c) Your life at particular moments, e.g. ten years ago, one year from now, etc., or at particular ages.
(d) Past, present and future self-images. Explore any conflicts of content.
(e) Concentrate on particular aspects of future, e.g. what job you would like, what sort of house, etc.
(f) Imagine yourself at a crossroads; what are your alternative directions?
(g) Decisions made/to be made.
(h) Changes and hopes for the New Year (etc.).
(i) Things that may be difficult in the near future.
(j) Scale of states from 'ideal' to 'rock-bottom'. Mark where you are now and the steps needed to move upwards. Perhaps link with No. 91 (Lifelines) to see what patterns have influenced you.
(k) Yourself at this moment in the context of past and future life.
(l) Personal coat of arms with spaces for specific information, e.g. hope for next year.
(m) Feelings of leaving one experience and going to another.
(n) Ideal world.
(o) Where I came from, where I am now and where I am going.
(p) Unfinished business.
(q) Regrets, and how you would have liked things to be.

(r) Losses you have suffered in your life, and what you would like to find in the future. See also No. 100.

(s) People important to you, or important in the past.

(t) Before and after: draw yourself or your life and how you felt before and after a particular event, e.g. accident, becoming ill, getting married, moving house, etc.

94. Life Collage

Pick out from magazines pictures that are relevant to your life (10 minutes), cut out words (5 minutes) and put together into collage representing your life (30 minutes).

Variations:

(a) Cut out a headline relevant to you and your life.

(b) Arrange the objects in your pocket/handbag according to the emotional distance from you and each other, to make a pattern of your life.

(c) Draw your concerns and arrange on paper to form 'life-space' picture.

(d) Pick out 3-5 pictures which make a statement about you, or show things you are willing to share.

95. Life Priorities Collage

On a large piece of paper, paint three horizontal bands of colour to represent far, middle and near distances. Then cut out or draw pictures to represent different aspects of your work, family and social life (or just one of these, e.g. social life). Stick these pictures on to the appropriate band of colour with rubber cement or other 'removable' adhesive. When you have finished, reflect on the results and move pictures around until the whole feels 'comfortable'. Useful in trying to reassess priorities.

96. Aspects of Self

Make a map with yourself in the centre, and place different aspects of yourself around the centre in relationship to one another, bearing in mind distance, size, etc.

Variations:

(a) Map of important things, places and people in your life, in relation to yourself.

(b) Three bands of colour for spiritual, mental and physical aspects. Discuss colour, textures, widths of bands in group, or pair up with someone with similar pattern.

(c) Mandala (centred image) of different aspects of self from centre outwards (see also No. 256).

(d) 'Community' of selves. Depict your various roles (e.g. car-driver, housewife, etc.) as a community on one piece of paper.

97. Recent Events

Think back over last week/night and represent something that made you happy, and then something upsetting.
Variations: Depict events of last week in strip cartoon form.

98. Childhood Memories

Draw your first or early memory, any childhood memory, or a memory which made a deep impression. These themes often bring up hurts from childhood that people have been unaware of, and can be difficult to deal with. It is important to allow enough time for discussion of these.
Variations:
(a) A warm or happy childhood memory and an unhappy one.
(b) A good memory and a bad one.
(c) An embarrassing moment.
(d) Yourself as a child.
(e) Memories associated with strong feelings.
(f) Paint first memory with other hand from the usual one.
(g) Talk and paint like children of 6-10, using fingerpainting.
(h) Write name in paint, first with right hand and then with left hand.
(i) Things you were not allowed in childhood. (Are these the things you feel most guilty about as an adult?)
(j) Draw memory as if at that age.
(k) 'Melting mirror' — a technique to reach back to childhood imaginatively. As you look at yourself in a mirror, it seems to melt and the image wavers. When it settles it reveals you as a child in a room in your house (settle on any age that seems to suggest itself). Imagine the room and a conversation between you and your child-self. What does the child say to you? What do you reply? Paint the situation, then see if there are any messages in it for you now.
(l) First memory of separation and present-day 'hellos' and 'goodbyes'. (Are there any connections?) This can bring up strong feelings.

99. Life Review

Draw or paint significant memories from your life. This can be useful for elderly people or those at a crossroads, in reviewing their lives. Some examples:
(a) Images from childhood, adolescence and adulthood.
(b) A good memory and a bad one.
(c) An embarrassing moment.
(d) Memories associated with strong feelings.
(e) Important events, e.g. weddings, births, deaths, leaving home, etc.
(f) Important groups of people, e.g. family, friends, village, workmates, war comrades, etc.

(g) City scenes and country scenes.
(h) Use old family photographs to build up picture album of life and events.
(i) Important ingredients of life, e.g. pets, houses, job, hobbies, activities specially enjoyed. Any of these can also be developed into longer projects.
(j) Daily life now and several years ago, and associated feelings.
(k) Depict family, friends, etc. with whom you have left something unsaid or unfinished. Add what you would have wished to say or do.
(l) Pass round objects from a previous era, such as household items, tools, etc. These can be a stimulus for many memories. (Members of the group may be able to contribute objects for this.)

100. Losses

Draw a picture or abstract symbol of someone or something which has gone.
Variations: Feelings surrounding this event.
This theme may be very cathartic and should be used with care, especially if people have suffered recent significant losses; but it may provide a valuable starting point for sharing important feelings. It can also be useful for elderly people suffering more gradual losses of physical abilities.

101. Secrets and Privacy

Depict, realistically or abstractly, three things:
(i) to be shared by the group;
(ii) perhaps to be shared;
(iii) not to be shared.
In the discussion, people may decide after all to share (ii) and (iii), but there should be no pressure to do so.
Variations:
(a) The private you and the shared you.
(b) The part you show to the world, and the part you do not show.
(c) See also No. 83.
(d) Being alone; being with others.
(e) Masks, or series of masks, for any of above. No pressure to share private masks. See also No. 102.

102. Public and Private Masks

Using a prepared mask, draw your face that you 'put on' in the morning for the world to see. Then draw a more private face that not many people see. Hold up each over your face and talk about yourself with your different 'faces' on. This exercise allows people to choose their own level of privacy to expose, and this should be respected; most people find it threatening to expose themselves too deeply in a group.

103. *Good and Bad*

Depict your good side and bad side; things you like and dislike about your-self; or things you would like to keep or change; or strengths and weaknesses, etc.

Variations:

(a) Clay shapes of aspects liked and disliked.
(b) Masks that represent ideal and unacceptable sides.
(c) Ideal self and real self.
(d) Look at negative and positive aspects in a painting and have a conversation with both parts.
(e) Changes made and to be made.
(f) Use paper bag for faces on both sides.

104. *Conflicts*

Depict any kind of conflict. Or more specifically, conflicting parts of your personality.

Variations:

(a) Animated metaphor of parts of personality in a cartoon strip.
(b) Depict any present conflict, and your parents sorting out their conflicts.
(c) Draw or model two opposing aspects of your personality. Give them voices and make up a dialogue. See also No. 265.

105. *Problems*

Portray any current problem, especially if it is persistent or recurrent. Then do another picture, or a collage of any benefits of having the problem.

106. *Emotions*

Paint different emotions and moods, using lines, shapes or colours. The emotions can be selected by the group.

Variations:

(a) Select pairs of opposites, e.g. love/hate, anger/calm, and combine into one picture.
(b) Quick abstract drawings in response to a spoken word, e.g. 'love', 'hate', 'anger', 'peace', 'work', 'family', etc.
(c) Start on even note, doodling with crayon, then express strong negative emotion (e.g. anger), then finish in opposite mood.
(d) Paint as many emotions as you can think of.
(e) Select one emotion for a theme painting, e.g. fear.
(f) Make a mask to express particular emotion.
(g) Mark different emotions in circle and put colours to them. Week by week take each one and do a separate picture.

(h) Draw objects associated with pleasant or unpleasant feelings or memories.
(i) Situations, involving other people, in which you have felt angry, anxious and peaceful.
(j) Paint a 'crazy' picture (as if you were crazy).
(k) Cut out magazine pictures for particular emotions, e.g. angry people, and imagine what they might be saying.
(l) Use clay to express strong feelings and make an 'angry object', using tools to cut, hammer, bash clay, etc.

107. Present Mood

Paint a picture of your mood or feelings at the moment. If appropriate, depict a metaphor, e.g. 'I'm all at sea', 'Everything's blank', etc.
Variations:
(a) Use marks, shapes, colours to represent physical and emotional feelings of moment.
(b) Use symbol to express current mood.
(c) Use doodles.
(d) Select one or more and paint picture of 'I am', 'I feel', 'I have', 'I do'.
(e) Paint recent or recurring problem of feeling. See also No. 105.
(f) Paint a pleasant feeling and an unpleasant feeling.
(g) Feelings of leaving one experience and going to another.
(h) Use for physical pain, e.g. headache, backache, etc.
(i) Do drawing of how you feel now. Then exaggerate that feeling, or part of the drawing, into a series of further drawings.

108. Objects and Feelings

Look at an object (flower, leaf, shell, etc.) for two minutes, then draw your feelings about it.
Variations:
(a) Look for longer period.
(b) Use only colours, lines and shapes.

109. Survival Needs

After an imaginative journey (see Section K) involving shipwreck on a desert island, paint a picture of your island, considering topography, means of survival, length of stay, etc.
Variations:
(a) Place yourself on a desert island with the things most important for your survival. What would you leave behind?
(b) Draw all the things you need — and then all the things you want.
(c) Create your own island and indicate the activities and people there.
(d) Use a folder as a 'suitcase' to take a few important things if home

endangered. Put address on it. Useful especially if this resonates with people's (or their relatives') experience.

110. Wishes

Paint one wish, three or five wishes. (More wishes demands greater imagination and can stretch people beyond conventional wishes.)
Variations:
(a) A journey you would like.
(b) Where I would like to be right now.
(c) Fantasy adventure in cartoon strip, including yourself.
(d) What would you do with £1 million?
(e) What would you have from a fantasy shop window?
(f) What would you like to find in a treasure chest?
(g) What would you like to find in an attic (and put in it)?
(h) Your hero/heroine.
(i) Illustrate an important hope and fear.
(j) A present you would like to receive (or give) and from whom?
(k) You are crossing a river. What is on the other side?
(l) You are a seed beginning to grow. What is the environment?
(m) Imagine a refuge which is a secure tranquil place. What is it like, and who is with you? What are the stresses and strains you would like to escape from?

111. Fears

Paint worst fear or one fear, three fears or five fears (see comment under No. 110).
Variations:
(a) Imagine you are hiding — where and from what?
(b) Threatening situations.
(c) You are adrift in a boat — what would you do?
(d) You are lost in a forest — what would you do?
(e) You are locked in a prison — how would you get out?
(f) Imagine a door or a gate — what lies behind it?

112. Pictorial Narratives

Explore a theme in narrative form, by telling a story in a number of frames, like a comic strip, with or without words. (It is a good idea to draw in the frames first or beforehand, e.g. divide the paper into nine equal rectangles or squares.) The story can occupy as many frames as seems appropriate.
Some examples:
(a) Tell a story about the journey of your life/your life script.
(b) Tell a story about what makes you tense/afraid.
(c) You are lost/adrift in a boat/in prison — what happens?
(d) Tell a story about where you would wish to be in life.

(e) Tell a story about the benefits of work, other than money.
(f) Tell a story of what happens when you come to the end of a journey.
(g) You are on a trip in an isolated area when your car gets stuck. What would you do?

Many of the themes in this section can be adapted to this form, which encourages people to put themselves in the story as the central character (although not always) and 'own' their actions and feelings. It is also a manageable and culturally accepted visual form for those who find the idea of 'painting pictures' strange and difficult. It can be particularly useful in helping people to come to terms with life crises, and plan viable futures. For children, it can be useful to make comic strips (or series of stick-on labels) about people or animals who undergo similar experiences or emotions to their own, e.g:

(h) Make up a picture story of a little dog who got lost.

It can also be helpful for the leader or therapist to supply an appropriate 'happy ending'. Anyone wishing to know more about this method should consult '*The Origins of Pictorial Narrative and Its Potential in Adult Psychiatry*' by Michael Donnelly (see Bibliography for address).

113. Likes and Dislikes

Depict a person you dislike, and how she/he sees you. Then do the same for a person you like. Possibly compare qualities with yourself.
Variations:
(a) Draw disliked person, then do what you will to it — tear up, etc.
(b) Pick out faces you like and dislike and make a collage (see also No. 116).
(c) Make clay shapes for likes and dislikes.
(d) Describe your best friend, then see how many qualities apply to you.
(e) Divide paper into six or eight sections and depict someone you admire, hate, love, pity, would like to change places with, who is often on your mind, etc.
(f) Draw something you like about yourself.
(g) Pick out pictures of same-sex people you admire, and make a collage.

114. Friendship Series

Portray:
(i)   a friend of the past;
(ii) the qualities of a friend;
(iii) a future friend.
Discussion of friendship, loneliness, etc.

115. Perceptions of Self and One Other

Draw an abstract image of yourself and one other important person.
Variations:

(a) Select two coloured shapes to represent self and other.
(b) Restrict choice of other person to inside or outside group.
(c) Ideal partner and imaginary opponent.
(d) Paint from standpoint of particular role, e.g. child, madman, etc.

116. *Shadow of Self*

Arrange a group of cut-out photographs of faces disliked (or liked) with the most disliked (or liked) in the centre of the group. Can use Gestalt technique with result (see Part One, Chapter 2, Section 12).
Variations:
(a) Draw image/symbol of characteristics thought most opposed to one's own. Identify with and discuss reactions to doing so.
(b) Note characteristics of same-sex persons who affect you negatively (e.g. parents, peers). Collect magazine pictures to represent these, and paste on sheet with most negative central to the group. Live with collage for a week, then start dialogue with it.
(c) Synthesise negative characteristics in picture. Can use Gestalt technique with result.
(d) Draw someone you hate in his or her most vile manifestations. Afterwards, try to recognise that this is a self-portrait. This is a way to discover unacceptable disowned portions of the self which are projected on to others.

117. *Anima/Animus*

Select magazine pictures related to both very positive and very negative feelings towards the opposite sex.
Variations:
(a) Draw images of your:
    (i) animus and anima;
    (ii) good and bad sides.
    Compare and discuss, especially if rigid demarcations result.
(b) Draw person, then person of opposite sex.
(c) Draw how you imagine you would feel if you were the opposite sex.
(d) Male/female — what do you consider are their different roles/characteristics?

118. *Introvert/Extrovert*

List or draw imagined qualities of person of opposite temperament to yourself (i.e. introverts list imagined qualities of extrovert), then paint as if you had one or more of these qualities.

119. *Personal Space*

Select your own size of paper and draw yourself somewhere on it.
Variations:

(a) choose colour and size of paper, and write your name on it. Decorate the rest if you wish.
(b) After choosing size, provide standard size paper and see if anyone asks for larger or smaller size paper.
(c) Draw yourself in (outer) space.

120. Personal Landscape

Draw a landscape (town, sea or countryside) and relate it to you personally.
Variations:
(a) Draw window of any size. Show view through window and what is in room. Realistic or abstract. (Results are sometimes looking out, sometimes looking in.)
(b) Take imaginary pictures with shoebox camera, focusing on what is significant in room.
(c) Paint yourself in a landscape.
(d) Paint an ideal or favourite place (or one disliked).

121. Personal Progression

Draw a picture that answers the question 'Who are you?' and try to make progressively more meaningful pictures each time in answer to the question. Write a description of each picture.

122. Time Progression

Portray the people in your life that influence you, during the first week of therapy, a course, etc. Repeat three or four months later.

123. Before and After Masks

Members of the group draw or paint a mask as they arrive at the group, then put it on one side, face down. At the end of the session, they draw another mask, then compare the two and discuss any changes in feelings and perceptions.

124. Mask Diary

Similar to No. 123 above, but 'before' and 'after' masks are drawn throughout the life of the group and put away in a folder. Towards the end of the sessions, they are spread out and each person shares their journey through their masks. In an ongoing group, a good time to share the masks would be after 5-8 weeks.

125. Reviewing Art Work

Look back at paintings and other art work done over a period of time, and notice any patterns, recurring themes. Also make any new projections that seem relevant but were not seen at the time.

126. Institutions

There are many themes which are concerned with reactions to arriving at, or being in, an institution, whether a school, hospital or prison (whether as a client or a member of staff). They are best tailored to particular needs and institutions. The examples below can be used with clients or staff:

(a) Experiences of first day or first impressions there.
(b) Story of how you came to be there, or in trouble. Can be taken on many levels.
(c) Main concerns, personal or institutional.
(d) How you see yourself, and how others see you, and how you would like to be seen.
(e) Your institution with yourself in it.
(f) Fold paper in half. Draw your life inside on one half, outside on the other half, and compare.
(g) Your professional self/role. See also (d) above.
(h) Your professional/client relationships (for staff).
(i) A 'rock-bottom' experience, and present situation. This focuses on feelings of powerlessness and loss of control.
(j) Situations and feelings which lead up to particular crises, e.g. drinking bout, criminal offence, overdose, etc.
(k) Your goals in your particular institution.
(l) When leaving: feelings about leaving and what your experience here has meant to you.
(m) What your institution does for you; what it does not do for you.
(n) Portrait (realistic or abstract) of leader, therapist, teacher; this brings out feelings towards her/him and towards institution.
(o) Feelings about approaching festivals (which may reinforce feelings of isolation, frustration, etc.).
(p) Comic strip of what you would do if you could leave the institution for a few days.

G *Family Relationships*

Many ideas in other sections can be adapted to 'family' use. The ones given here are specific to families. They are in two subsections:

(i)   Perceptions of Family — individual exercises about family relationships, and
(ii) Families in Action — group activities for families to examine the way they relate in the present.

Perceptions of Family

How we perceive our relationships with our families. Most people have strong feelings about their families, so sensitivity will be needed in introducing these, and it is important to allow plenty of time for discussion. Some of these themes can be particularly difficult for certain groups of people, e.g. the recently bereaved or those who have been orphans.

127. Family Portraits

Portraits can be either realistic or use any of the devices in Section J, Nos. 197, 198, 204 or 205. One method is to describe, as if to a stranger on a train, the others in your family and how to recognise them. These can then be portrayed in paint or clay.
Variations:
(a) Self-portrait using same method.
(b) Members of family as animals or objects (see No. 204).
(c) Simply draw your family.
(d) Carry on dialogue between family members in painting.
(e) Cut out pictures which remind you of your family.

128. Kinetic Family Drawings

Draw your family with all the members doing something, or the family as a whole doing something or going somewhere, or a scene from family life.
Variations:

(a) Specify more closely, e.g. a day out with family, etc.
(b) The role you play in your family.
(c) Given a house plan, put in family members and describe the activities.

129. *Family Sculpture of Relationships*

Represent your family relationships by modelling each member in a characteristic position in relation to others. This can be done with clay, or using a live group of people.
Variations:
(a) Sociogram illustrating self in relation to family using size of circle and distance apart to signify importance and emotional distance.
(b) Family mobile: 3-D sociogram using coat-hanger, cardboard and string.
(c) Family tree; family as a tree with a part assigned to each member, or family members in characteristic positions on branches, according to distance from self. (Imagine going to sleep in a tree and waking to find members of your family or those close to you all saying 'Hello'. Paint their positions — near you perhaps, or even falling out of the tree. Good for children.)

130. *Inheritance*

Fold paper in four, and depict in each section:
(i) what you have inherited;
(ii) what you would have liked to inherit;
(iii) what you most disliked inheriting;
(iv) what you would like your children to inherit.
Variations:
(a) Family past, present and as you would like it to be.
(b) Strengths and weaknesses received from each parent.

131. *Family Comparisons*

Select a relevant theme from Section F (Self-perceptions) and after doing it for yourself, repeat for others in your family, e.g. mother, father, spouse, children, etc. Are there any similarities?

132. *Childhood Memories*

Do a family sculpture (see No. 129) representing a time during your childhood. Childhood memories often remind people of long-forgotten hurts, which can be upsetting. It is important to be aware of this, and allow time for their expression.
Variations:
(a) Imaginative journey to childhood to bring back memories (see also No. 98).
(b) Paint yourself now, the things you like, body image, occupations, etc.;

then do the same for some point in your childhood.
(c) Make dolls' houses representing various stages of identification, e.g. grandparents, parents, children's home, etc.

133. Re-enacting Parental Relationships

Split into two groups — 'parents' and 'children'. Do various role plays emphasising relationship, e.g. blind walks, rocking, etc. Then 'children' draw pictures for 'parents', who provide the materials; 'parents' play with 'children' or do a picture for them. Discussion on parent/child relationship.
Variations:
(a) Draw your mother (father) criticising you (or similar statement according to situation).
(b) Fingerpaint to Transactional Analysis statements made by leader ('parent', 'adult' or 'child' statements, e.g. 'Go to your room', 'I appreciate your opinion', 'Let's play'). For an introduction to Transactional Analysis, see *I'm O.K. — You're O.K.* by T.A. Harris (Pan Books, London, 1973).
(c) Paint the group as a family, allocating roles.

134. Family Themes

There are any number of themes which can be invented to stimulate memories, feelings, discussion about families, e.g:
(a) Yourself and one other member of the family.
(b) A memory from your childhood.
(c) You and your parents, etc.
(d) Family events, e.g. weddings, births, deaths, gatherings, etc.

135. Family Relationships Through Play

Children often find it difficult to articulate their feelings in a direct way, but can enact situations through other means (see also Part One, Chapter 1), e.g:
(a) Sand play. Use sandbox and miniature figures of animals and people to portray situations and tell stories, which may have a bearing on family life.
(b) Paper figures. Fold and cut paper dolls and animals, evolving stories about animal and human families as you proceed.
(c) Use play dough (see No. 39 for recipes) to make figures of importance to the child, and see what they do and say.
(d) Use a family of dolls to describe situations and feelings.

Families in Action

These ideas are for families or couples to explore their actual relationships;

for instance, in family therapy sessions. Some of these exercises can enable quiet family members to make an equal contribution. However, they may thus uncover truths that some family members find difficult to accept. Support may be needed to help these families come to terms with what is revealed and, if appropriate, to find new ways of relating to each other.

136. Realistic Family Portraits

Each person draws a picture of the family, making full figures (rather than stick figures) of all individuals, including oneself.

137. Abstract Family or Marital Relationship

Each person draws at the same time, on separate sheets of paper, an abstract or symbolic picture of the family or marital relationship.

138. Emotional Portraits

Mother and father (or husband and wife) draw emotional portraits of each other. They then swap pictures and change their portraits as they would like them to be.
Variation: Make large realistic self-portraits, give to partner to change as wished.

139. Present Situation

All members of the family draw pictures of the situation now, and as they would like to see it. Looking at the differences can help families set their own goals for change.

140. Important Things

Families draw at home those things most important to them, and bring their drawing along to the next session for discussion.

141. Shared Experience

Each member of the family draws a picture of her/himself and what she/he was doing at the weekend. These are compared and discussed.
Variations:
(a) Other scenes from family life.
(b) See Kinetic Family Drawings, No. 128.
(c) Use any theme from Perceptions of Family subsection, and compare pictures.

142. Problems and Problem-solving

Each member of the family depicts the prevalent problem in their family and how it has affected their life as an individual, e.g. alcohol, criminal offences, mental illness, overdoses, disability, unemployment, etc.
Variation: If there is a particular problem facing a family, or one member

of it, each person depicts how they view the problem, their needs, etc. and their feelings about it. The different views are then discussed and if possible a course of action clarified.

143. Anger

Members of the family each draw a picture related to their anger. They are then asked to give it to another member of the family.

144. Parents and Children

Children draw pictures of themselves when younger. Parents draw pictures of themselves at ages similar to one of their children. This may bring out similar roles, problems, projections, identifications, etc.

145. Boss-Slave

See No. 170, with child bossing mother or father.

146. Single-parent Families

Each member of the family does a drawing or collage to show the good and bad things about having one parent at home/being a single parent.

147. Grandparents' Influence

This is in two parts:
(i) Each member of family draws symbolic picture of family (see No. 137).
(ii) Divide paper in half. On one side, draw symbolic picture of maternal grandparents' family; on the other side, paternal grandparents' family. After completion, mark which of the two more nearly resembles the picture done in (i).

This exercise can be useful in tracing unconscious heritage from previous generations.

148. Family Sculpture in Action

See No. 129, but in the present, using family members.

149. Family Drawing or Painting

The family members draw or paint together on one large sheet of paper. They then discuss the family dynamics.
Variations:
(a) Family first decides what painting will be about.
(b) Joint construction project, using any materials.

150. Sharing Resources

A family is given a set of materials to create a family sculpture. The materials can include various things such as a cardboard base, scissors, glue, oil pastels and sheets of stiff paper of different colours, but there should be fewer sheets of paper than members of the family, so that they have to decide how to allocate resources (e.g. four sheets for family of five).

151. Teams

Each member of the family chooses a different colour crayon or marker. Family divides into two teams, and each team produces a picture by the members taking turns, in silence. This may pick up 'family alliances' and the way they work.

152. Art Evaluation Session

This is a series developed by art therapists working in family and marital therapy. Spend about 10 minutes on each task, followed by 10-15 minutes' discussion. This series is based on work by H. Kwiatkowska.
(a) Realistic family portrait, see No. 136.
(b) Abstract family or marital relationship, see No. 137.
(c) Joint scribble, see No. 158(f).
(d) Self-portrait given to partner, see No. 138.
(e) Individual pictures, no subject given.

153. Other Pair or Group Activities

Use any of the pair or group activities in Sections H, I and J, as appropriate. These may be revealing, but also a source of shared enjoyable activity which can be important for families.

For further details of couple and family techniques see *Family Therapy and Evaluation Through Art* by H. Kwiatkowska (C.C. Thomas, Springfield, Illinois, 1978), *Clinical Art Therapy* by Helen Landgarten (Brunner/Mazel, New York, 1981) and *Art Psychotherapy* by Harriet Wadeson (John Wiley, New York and Chichester, 1980).

H   *Working in Pairs*

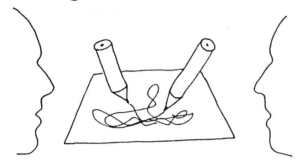

This section includes games and exercises requiring pairs. Many of these are about the relationship between the pair, and there are several variations in the 'ground rules' which affect the interaction. For most of them it is best to work in silence, letting the painting/drawing, etc. take the place of words.

154. Drawing and Painting in Pairs

Paint in pairs on the same piece of paper. If having no other rules is too daunting, try the effect of some different rules, e.g:
(a) One person draw curves, the other straight lines.
(b) Each person sticks to a certain colour or colours.
(c) Each mirrors what the other draws, simultaneously.

155. Conversations

Choose a colour which expresses an aspect of yourself, and silently pair up with someone who has a different colour. Then have a conversation in paint or crayons on the same paper, each using one colour, one at a time, keeping to your own line.
Variations:
(a) Use colours and shapes, any sort of marks, and reply to them.
(b) Stipulate kind of conversation, e.g. getting angry.
(c) One person at a time, while other watches, then other starts where first person left off.
(d) Both work simultaneously taking own lines for a walk.
(e) Following each other.
(f) Exchange colours after a while.
(g) Develop into shared drawing.
(h) Use opposite hand from usual one.
(i) With pairs on opposite sides of a long sheet of paper, start conversation with opposite person, then develop conversation with neighbours on either side.

156. Painting with an Observer

One member of a pair says what comes to mind as she/he watches another paint. The painter responds as she/he sees fit.
Variation:
Watcher mirrors artist's rhythm and way of working. Can also have third person observing both. Rotate roles.

157. Sharing Space

Start by taking turns on the same paper, then continue by drawing simultaneously. Look at the way you have structured the space.
Variations:
(a) Select three colours between you and draw the experience of your relationship, especially how you are sharing the space.
(b) Exchange colours after a while.
(c) Use collage methods, each person has different colour sticky paper to make pattern on large sheet in common.

158. Joint Pictures

Do a picture with a partner, preferably in silence. Respond to each other's communications and maintain the relationship while painting. Good for meeting new people and for the risk-taking involved.
Variations:
(a) Simply paint in pairs in silence.
(b) Create an environment for both to exist in.
(c) Start with own colour and eyes closed for two minutes, then work together on result.
(d) Agree on a theme beforehand.
(e) Work with partner to produce a picture which is a cohesive whole.
(f) Each partner makes own scribble, with eyes closed. Then both make associations with results and decide on one scribble to develop into a picture. When the picture is complete, make up a story about it.

159. Winnicott Squiggles (based on the work of D.W. Winnicott)

Do a squiggle, then swap with partner, who tries to make an image out of it. Good for 'warming up' or for getting imagination going when a group is stuck or flagging.
Variations:
(a) Paint a symbol or representation of a current moment or concern. Swap silently with partner and continue on his/hers, not obliterating anything. Discuss interplay of interpretations and fantasy.
(b) Draw something and then exchange to work on partner's. Can be theme-oriented or anything that comes to mind.

160. Introduction Interviews

Interview partner and then make picture to show something about partner's life and concerns.

161. Dialogue

Paint something to express a current feeling or concern. Partner paints something in response. Reverse roles and repeat.
Variations:
(a) Partners each work on own part of picture simultaneously, then swap to respond.
(b) Draw problem on left, exchange, partner draws solution on right.
(c) Dangerous journey. One person draws a path and a hazard, other person draws solution.

162. Sequential Drawings

First person draws characters, second person writes dialogue, etc., to create continuous story.
Variation: First and second persons take turns drawing to create story, no written dialogue.

163. Portraits

Draw a self-portrait and a portrait of your partner. This results in four portraits altogether, which are then shared and discussed.
Variations:
(a) Portrait of partner in colours and shapes.
(b) Draw self-portrait, then exchange with partner for further additions; draw portrait of partner and exchange for additions.
(c) Draw your partner, looking when not drawing.
(d) After drawing portraits, interview your partner.
(e) Pay special attention to details such as buttons, belts, etc.
(f) Use collage to get different effects.

164. First Impressions

Similar to Portraits (see No. 163). Relax and look at each other. On a shared piece of paper, take turns to draw anything to which eyes are attracted in partner's face, without lifting crayon from paper. Discuss results when finished.
Variations:
(a) On shared paper, take turns to put down first impressions, thoughts or feelings, using abstract means.
(b) Paint impressions of partner using one shape and one colour.
(c) Paint portrait of partner's face, giving an impression of the sort of person.

(d) Paint pictures of the sort of person you are for your partner, and the sort of person she/he is for you.
(e) Make portraits of each other, and below them write affirmative statements about partner.

165. *Masks*

Make a mask (or use a prepared blank mask) and paint on it an impression of your partner while she/he is wearing it.
Variations:
(a) Make and paint a mask, or several masks. Work with partner, trying on masks.
(b) See also Masks (No. 86); do these in pairs.
(c) Make masks for each other of the 'front(s)' the other person wears. (It is sometimes easier for others to be aware of our 'fronts' than we are ourselves.)
(d) Use collage materials or 'media images' cut from magazines.

166. *Face Painting*

Similar to Masks, but using the 'real thing'! In pairs, paint your partner's face with your impression of what sort of person she/he is.
Variation: Using your partner's face as a canvas, paint an abstract design or expressive mask, taking your time.

167. *Silhouettes*

Using a piece of paper and a lamp, work in pairs to draw round each other's shadows. Draw in details on partner's silhouette.
Variations:
(a) Move about to notice different shadows in different positions.
(b) Simply fill in own silhouette in black.
(c) With children, if the whole room is darkened, those waiting for their turn can work on clay or something else, enjoying and coming to terms with the 'scary' atmosphere.

168. *Relationships*

Use any combination of warm-up games, followed by both partners painting on a chosen personal theme from Section F (Self-perceptions); the resulting paintings are then shared. Finally, draw or paint the relationship you have built up with your partner, either individually or together.

169. *Joint Project*

Undertake a joint activity with your partner, e.g. drawing, painting, collage, sculpture, building something. Conversation encouraged.
Variation: Jointly make object from junk materials, no speaking.

170. Boss-Slave

One person tells the other which art materials to use, how to use them and what to paint/draw, etc. Reverse roles. Discuss experience. This will bring up issues of control and authority. Particularly useful in providing situation in which roles can be reversed from normal ones, e.g. child bosses parent or teacher.

I   *Group Paintings*

All the items in this section are group paintings in which several people contribute jointly to one piece of paper or one finished product. The differences between group paintings lie in the 'ground rules' set out, and each of the ideas below has selected a different set of these rules, which then influences what happens. (The type of group, setting, environment, etc. also influences what happens, of course. See Chapter 2 in Part One.) As well as showing individuals' perceptions, group paintings often reveal very powerfully (and sometimes painfully) some of the group dynamics operating.

Some useful questions which may be asked about group interaction:

How does the art form get started?

Who takes the initiative?

Whose suggestions are used? Ignored?

Do people take turns, form teams or work simultaneously?

Is anyone left out?

Where is each person's work situated, and how much space is used?

Do people add to others' work?

Who is the leader or most active participant?

What influence do different kinds of boundary have?

Is group painting an enjoyable or a threatening experience?

Not all of these are relevant or beneficial to every situation, it depends how much exploration is seen as valuable. Photograph 18 shows a staff group at a mental hospital at work on a group painting.

171. Group Painting with Minimal Instructions

At its most basic, a group is simply presented with a huge sheet of paper (on floor or tables) and asked to work as a group on one large picture with no specified theme. Many of the questions at the beginning of this section will be relevant to the discussion.

Variations which may be used to add the desired amount of structure to this situation:

(a) Each person selects one colour and keeps it; or changes it later if desired; or negotiates with others for colours to mix with the first one.

18: Group Painting in Process — Staff Group at Mental Hospital

(Photograph by John Ford)

(b) All start painting at same time.
(c) Work in teams.
(d) Work co-operatively.
(e) Theme can be decided by group or arrived at in the course of the painting.
(f) All start in centre of paper, or all start at edge of paper.
(g) Take turns for two minutes each, then 'free for all'.
(h) Use fingers and hands

172. Co-operative Painting

Huge group painting on unspecified theme, but working in with each other, linking own part to neighbour's part. Build up shared experience.
Variation: Discuss effects of framework and rules (see above); do they help or hinder growth of group experience?

173. Wall Newspaper

Provide a large sheet of paper on the wall, plus felt-tip pens (tied on with string!). Anyone can write or draw anything at any time. Good for letting off steam and expressing ideas anonymously (e.g. at a conference).

174. A Cohesive Whole

Each person draws a picture for ten minutes on an individual piece of paper. When the pieces of paper are turned over, they have numbers and letters on, e.g. 1A, 1B ... 3C, 3D, etc. These are sellotaped in a grid:

   1A 1B 1C 1D
   2A ....
   3A .... etc.

The complete set is turned over once more and the group has to make the picture into a cohesive whole, without talking.

Variation: On a large piece of paper, each person makes a spontaneous scribble. The group then makes a cohesive whole out of these.

175. Moving On

Everyone starts around a huge piece of paper, does some painting or drawing, and then moves on one place.

176. Picking Out Images

The group covers the paper with spontaneous colours and shapes. Then the paper is passed around and members pick out images they see and emphasise them by drawing them in.

Variations: Talk about one of the shapes (liked or disliked) in the first person.

177. Own Territories

Members draw out their own territories, mark them with their names and put in something of themselves. Then everyone is free to put anything else into other people's territorial spaces. Discussion can include who gave what to whom, etc.

Variations:

(a) Give other people something you think they need.
(b) Allow 10-15 minutes for initial claiming of areas, and finish by returning to own area to make final changes or additions.
(c) After working on initial territories containing selves, link up with other territories.

178. Group 'Mandala'

On a large sheet of paper, draw a large circle and divide it into sectors like pieces of cake, according to the number of people in the group. Individuals can decide whether they wish to remain in their own territories, portraying anything they wish, or whether they also want to enter other people's spaces; individuals also decide whether their boundaries are to be firm or blended in with those of neighbours on either side. Discussion can

look at how people's decisions affected the whole painting and the interactions between people.
Variations:
(a) Divide large circle into smaller concentric rings, one for each person.
(b) Choose a theme for whole group, e.g. day and night.

179. Individual Starting Points

Each person takes one colour, and with eyes closed takes a line for a walk.
After a few minutes, everyone opens their eyes and develops their own
spaces with all colours, merging with others at the boundaries.
Variations:
(a) The initial stage can involve some moving around the paper.
(b) The later stages can include working on the picture as a whole.
(c) Discussion can be in the whole group, or include conversations with
    neighbours on the paper.
(d) Childhood version: choose an age between 5 and 18 before starting
    with own line and space.

180. Group Stories

Each person begins to paint a story somewhere on the paper, or from own
space. As everyone expands and comes across other people's stories, allow
these individual stories to develop and include others' aspects. Move
around the paper.
Variations:
(a) Move around the paper in turn to add to each story, until arriving back
    at your own.
(b) Depict common story or event around the paper.
(c) Start with drawing of 'where you feel you are' at edge of paper, then
    move on to continue others' stories.

181. Fairy Story in Time Sequence

Each person draws his/her own fairy story in time sequence, on a long
sheet of paper (initial agreement on top, bottom, beginning and end of
paper). Anyone can start anywhere. No talking.
Variations:
(a) Everyone writes a story or poem about the finished painting, and reads
    it out to the group.
(b) Further poems, stories or paintings inspired by the group painting.

182. One-word-at-a-time Story

Each person says a word in turn, to make up a story, which is written
down. This story is then illustrated either by individual paintings or by a
group painting.
Variations:

(a) Paint a story, using people's images to make the story grow.
(b) Pass a painting around, telling a story as you add to it.

183. One-at-a-time Group Drawing

On a large piece of paper, one person starts, others watching. Then the next continues, and so on.
Variations:
(a) Start with a story, next person continues.
(b) Make marks in response to what has gone before.
(c) Use only dots, straight lines or curves, first black and white, later perhaps using colours.
(d) Have a fixed number of turns, or stop by common consent.
(e) Pass paper round if small.
(f) Project into picture (if abstract) and draw fantasies of what is seen.
(g) Take turns with drawing something about yourself. Finally, add to whole if wished.
(h) Introductions: name plus picture of self, on sheet on wall.
(i) Theme murals: after discussion of theme, each person goes to mural in turn and draws.
(j) Use paints and blocks of colour rather than lines.
(k) Clay: pass round a lump of clay; each person does something quickly and then passes it on. Discuss feelings associated with changes.

184. Group Murals on Themes

These are murals — on large sheets of paper pinned to the wall or on black-boards — on specified themes which are chosen by the leader or the group, or arrived at by discussion or 'brainstorming'. They can be worked on by one person at a time or by the whole group simultaneously (provided the group is not too large).
Examples of themes:
(a) Facets of life at any particular centre, institution, etc.
(b) Group events, e.g. outing, picnic, party, etc.
(c) Feelings about a common experience to group.
(d) Fantasy themes such as travel, life under the sea, life in outer space, animals, etc.
(e) Abstract design.

185. Solidarity

Sometimes oppressed minorities can find it useful to celebrate their common bonds and their positive contributions, by drawing or painting murals depicting their experiences of these. There may be political issues involved, and these can generate heated arguments!
Examples of themes:
(a) Ethnic minority festivals and music.

(b) Women's contributions to humanity.
(c) Symbols of peace.
(d) Murals of local activities in the surrounding community.
(e) What elderly, disabled, etc. people have in common all over the world.

186. Building Islands and Worlds

The group uses a collection of junk materials, paint, collage, crayons, etc. to build an island or world for the group to live on.
Variations:
(a) If several small groups are doing this, they can later visit other islands to compare with their own.
(b) Instead of an island, build a park, school, community centre, town, city, world or 'group environment'.
(c) Use crayons or paint instead of junk materials.
(d) Specify more conditions, e.g. town on particular occasion, stranded on an island, aerial view of village with participants developing own areas and working or living communally.
(e) Draw individual islands on mural, then choose someone else's island to visit and devise means of getting there. If appropriate, discuss reasons for choice.
(f) Draw individual towns in corners of large sheet of paper, then make a road to someone else's town (best with groups of four).
(g) Create fantasy community on mural paper with markers or crayons.
(h) Create own house, and then make neighbourhood.
(i) Use clay to make clay 'world'.
(j) Create individual clay trees and make a forest on a large board. If outside, also add sticks, leaves and stones.
(k) Use collage to make circular 'world'.
(l) Worlds in boxes.
(m) Make full-length self-portrait and put in most suitable place for self. Group discusses and perhaps changes, then creates suitable environment for the self-portraits.
(n) If several groups are involved, final discussion can compare cities or worlds, or evolve criteria for evaluating them.
(o) Picture or sculpture of the group.

187. Group Collage

Many of the ideas listed so far can be translated into collage by using magazines and ready-made images instead of paints or crayons, e.g. using collage for a theme mural, making a world, etc.
Variation (good for children): Each child is given total control of at least one piece of equipment (e.g. scissors), which only she/he may use.

188. *Feelings Collage*

Cut out pictures which clearly express emotion, and paste into a collage. Write what each character might be saying.
Variation: Group members can mime or act the feelings expressed.

189. *Contributions*

The following are all ideas for group paintings which consist of individual contributions from group members. They are specially suitable for groups which would not be able to work together in a less structured way.
(a) Assembly of individual panels (previously prepared to fit together) on given themes, in crayon, paint or collage.
(b) Each person assigned a fixed space on a given project.
(c) Jigsaw: cut blank group shape into smaller shapes. Each members fills in one shape, then the larger shape is reassembled.
(d) A large piece of paper is divided into sections meeting at a central circle. Different shapes are assigned to each member, e.g. triangles, squares, stars, etc., with instructions to work towards and enter the centre.
(e) In a group, draw a tree — then everyone puts different things underneath.
(f) Draw a house, then different people put in different rooms and activities.
(g) Four people can use four sides of box to do individual contributions on any theme.
(h) Discuss how individual contributions are to be fitted together.

190. *Moving Closer*

For an ongoing group, if working on co-operative projects is difficult, devise stages in moving closer:
(a) Work in allotted space on large paper, physically distant from each other.
(b) Reduce allotted space to increase physical proximity.
(c) Unify individual parts to make a cohesive whole.
(d) All work on one small project, without allotting spaces.

191. *Group Sculptures*

The group works together on one piece of clay, with no set theme, or to produce a joint sculpture.
Variations:
(a) Use a layer of clay in same way as group painting (rather clay-consuming).
(b) Use other 3-D materials such as wood offcuts or junk materials.
(c) Good for children; each child has total control of at least one piece of

junk, clay, plasticine, etc., which only she/he can use to produce co-operative group sculpture.
(d) Everyone does a part of a particular scene (e.g. park, circus) and then makes it into a whole.
(e) Each person uses different colour of plasticine or other materials so that individual contributions can be seen.
(f) Each person has different materials, e.g. coloured paper, tissue paper, cellophane, etc. First person starts, passes on to next to add something, and so on.

192. Overlapping Group Transparency

This is good for a group which has worked together on another project or been together for some time. Each person chooses a different colour of cellophane and uses it to represent her/himself in the group, according to shape, size and position. Using coloured cellophane means that the way the group functions can also be shown, by overlapping the individual shapes.

193. Group Roles

Each person makes a three-dimensional self-image (in clay, plasticine, wood scraps or other junk materials), then moves it about in silence on a large piece of paper or board which acts as a 'world space'. When each person has found his or her 'spot', this is marked by a line drawing. Then the group discusses the various possible roles in a group, e.g. facilitator, disruptor, outsider, intruder, scapegoat, peacemaker, etc.

194. Role-playing

Group painting with people assigned different roles, preferably role reversals from usual behaviour. Finish by doing individual pictures to go back to 'being oneself'.

195. Painting to Music

Paint as a group to music, being aware of group and feelings.
Variations:
(a) Warm up by moving to music.
(b) Movement exercises, followed by painting, with movements of different qualities, e.g. bold, sweeping, controlled, etc.

196. Individual Response to Group Painting

Group paintings can be powerful experiences. These may be assimilated better if each member of the group does an individual painting in response to the group painting experience. These may be shared if desired.

J *Group Games*

This section includes exercises in which the rules for interaction presuppose a group, although there is no group end-product. These rules for interaction are like those of games, where a different rule makes a different game. Most of the games involve comparing one's own perceptions with those of others. Many of them extend ideas from Section F (Self-perceptions) and H (Working in Pairs). The game element can help to make them very enjoyable, and also give a new perspective on serious concerns.

197. *Portraits*

Make quick portraits of everyone else (e.g. ten portraits in 30 minutes); sign them and give them to the person drawn.
Variations:
(a) Suggest portraits should be funny/in shapes/using textures.
(b) Sketches of others in group walking or doing typical activity (can be matchstick figures).
(c) Clay figures: model the figure of another group member in posture that clearly communicates his/her feeling.
(d) Draw portraits of self using distinctive features; comment on own drawings to group. Group supplies nickname possibly. Or guess who drew portraits.

198. *Portraits by Combined Effort*

Each member is the subject in turn, and draws a self-portrait. Then other members in turn make the portrait more like the subject.

199. *Badges and Totems*

Paint a badge to describe yourself and pin it on yourself. Then make similar badges for others, describing their main characteristics. Works best when people know each other well, or in a group of people prepared to take risks.
Variations:

(a) Put individual badges on group 'totem pole'.
(b) Coats of arms for yourself and others.

200. Group Symbol

The group develops and paints a symbol which is shared by the whole group.
Variation: Group coat of arms.

201. Masks

Everyone paints a mask, then wears it and takes part in plays involving the mask's character; best done in small groups, say fours. There are many variations and ways of achieving the chosen masks, e.g:
(a) Mask of unacceptable side of your personality. Then get together in fours with opposite masks, forming a 'family unit' to do a role play. Imagination and visualisation techniques can be used to get in touch with the unacceptable side (see Section K).
(b) One person talks about his/her mask, and another person acts the role.
(c) Everyone brings an object to the group. Then each person does a mime using all the objects and evolves a 'character' which is then painted on his/her mask. The masks are then used in a play.
(d) Use paper bags and paint to make characters which come alive, and act plays with them (good for children).

202. Gifts

Make, draw or paint gifts you would like to give to each person in the group, and then give them. This can also be done on a large blackboard. Discussion will explore feelings around giving and receiving, and possibly around parting with the gifts.
Variations:
(a) To end a group, a 'goodbye' gift to take away.
(b) Can be geared to festivals, e.g. Christmas, Easter, etc.
(c) Stipulate kind of gift — concrete, abstract, etc.
(d) Can have particular purpose, e.g. to help attain a short-term goal.
(e) Precious objects.
(f) Can be repeated at intervals; see if gifts become more relevant.
(g) Make or draw any object, then give it to someone in the group.

203. Shared Feelings

Choose a topic of concern to group members, e.g. a shared problem, situation, etc. Each person draws good and bad things about the particular situation, each thing on a separate small piece of paper. Any shared images are then discussed as a set.

204. *Metaphorical Portraits: Individuals*

Paint metaphorical portraits of others (and self) in the group (see also No. 89). Sometimes there is only time for a few, sometimes everyone can do a portrait of everyone else. The portraits can be abstract or can be flowers, animals, buildings, trees, houses, islands, etc.

There are several ways of sharing the results;

(a) Everyone takes turns to explain the portraits they have done.
(b) One person holds up a portrait, others guess who it is; the person who guesses correctly then holds up a portrait, and so on.
(c) When each portrait has been discussed or 'guessed', it is given to the subject as a gift. At the end, everyone has a collection of metaphorical portraits of themselves.

Further variations of this idea:

(d) Self and one other — abstracts. This can be specified to be someone in the group or not in the group. The guessing game can then suggest who the other person is.
(e) Draw an imaginary animal, then see what happens when two animals meet.
(f) See also No. 89.

205. *Metaphorical Portrait: Group*

Find a metaphor for the group as a whole and paint it. This can be done separately by each individual, or as a group.

Variations:

(a) Draw the group as animals with a background.
(b) Draw yourself as part of the group, using colour, position, form, etc. This can be added to or changed over a period of time.
(c) Combine with No. 204. Portray members of group individually and the group as a whole.

206. *Interpretations*

The basic idea is to compare group interpretations with what was intended. There are many ways of doing this, e.g:

(a) See Nos. 204 and 205 (c) (metaphorical portraits of individuals and group). In discussion, everyone else (apart from artist) comments, makes associations and interpretations; artist keeps silent.
(b) Everyone paints a picture on a specified theme, e.g. a face, a tree, an animal, a house, an island, a mask, etc. The pictures are collected and shuffled, then held up one by one. The group describes each picture in a way that could describe a person.
(c) Everyone paints their ideas of different emotions, e.g. anger, anxiety, etc., and labels each small picture on the reverse. The pictures are mixed up, then the group picks one out and tries to agree on an interpretation. This is then compared with the original intention.

(d) One person describes a picture, which everyone tries to draw from the instructions. The completed pictures are compared with the original and discussion focuses on the different interpretations people make of information given to them.

(e) (For children) Each child gives a 'word' to another child to depict in some way. Discussion focuses on how children interpreted a particular word.

207. Interpretations in Action

In groups of three, each person paints a symbol or situation of the present. Swap silently and continue, not obliterating anything. Repeat with third person, then back to original. Discuss interpretations.

208. Conflict Cartoons

Groups of 2-5 people co-operate to produce a cartoon illustrating a conflict or theme they feel is important. Then each group passes their cartoon to another group for interpretation and consideration of bias, stereotypes, viewpoint offered, etc. (This is based on the fact that cartoons often rely on using stereotypes to communicate their message.)

209. Butterflies

Each person makes two 'butterflies' by folding sheets of paper in half on daubs of paint. Put one aside, and then do a mono-print of someone else's on top of your second one. Repeat with more interactions on the same one, as many as wished. Discuss fears of loss of identity in group; the clean butterfly can represent preserved identity.

210. Life-size Individuals and Group

Draw outline around each person, then fill in colours in outlines other than your own.
Variations:
(a) Put in characteristics of that person.
(b) Others in group put in hat, clothes, shoes, etc.

211. Round Robin Drawings

Number the papers around the group. Everyone draws for two minutes (this needs timing, preferably by a non-participant), then passes their paper on and continues on the next one for one minute; and so on until everyone receives back the one she/he started with and finishes it off for two minutes. No talking. Discussion focuses on people's feelings about the changes in their pictures. Sometimes useful for a new group, as no-one has to take responsibility for a whole picture.
Variations:
(a) Start by drawing for longer period, e.g. five minutes.

(b) Finish with longer period, e.g. five minutes.
(c) Specify starting point is something from own situation.
(d) Specify no obliterations.
(e) Reflect on results and do individual drawing to express feelings.
(f) Add a word each when painting is done.
(g) Close eyes, take a line for a walk, open eyes to do some drawing, then pass on to someone else.
(h) Specify a theme, e.g. 'having fun'.
(i) (For children) Child starts a drawing and asks next child to add to it according to their instructions, e.g. 'I've drawn a car; I'd like you to put some wheels on it'.

212. Fill in the Gap

Do a picture and leave something out; the leader has to guess what. Or leave something for someone else to do.
Variation:
(a) Use this to remind of last session, group and leader catch each other out if they forget anything.

213. Leader Draws

Group members tell leader what to draw. This gives group members permission to reveal feelings towards authority (leaders, parents, etc.), or allows normally passive members to be more active.

214. Beautiful and Ugly

First person makes something beautiful, and this is continued for several passings-on; then it is turned into something ugly; then made good again. Explore the feelings associated with each process. (People with very low esteem have difficulty with this one, as they may feel that all their drawings are ugly anyway. Also, some people simply cannot bear the idea of spoiling something on purpose.)
Variations:
(a) In groups of four, alternate members make beautiful, spoil, remake beautiful, etc. Finally, original artist makes it beautiful to finish. Allow five minutes each part.
(b) Two groups do a picture each, swap to spoil, then make good again.
(c) Each person does a second picture, including all the good and bad elements, and tries to make them into a 'whole' picture.

215. Secrets

Everyone draws a secret without saying what it is. Discuss what having a secret means. Swap paintings with another person, and do a sketch which is a parody of their secret. Discussion.

216. Pool of Drawings

Everyone begins drawing anything they like; when they feel like it, they place it in the middle of the circle and continue on someone else's drawing. This carries on until it comes to a natural conclusion.

217. Group Additions

Each member names an object, event or feeling and depicts it. Then other members add improvements. Discussion of feelings about the changes that are made.

218. Group Sequential Drawing

Divide a piece of paper into numbered squares, one more than the number of people in the group. In the first square draw the beginning of a story (for three minutes). Pass it on, and draw in the second square on the next paper. When everyone gets their own back, the end of the story is put in. Discussion.

Variations:

(a) Write very quick synopsis of story.
(b) Cut up sections and reassemble own sections, to see if they have any particular theme.
(c) Specify starting point, e.g. important event, childhood memory, etc.
(d) Captions: when papers are passed on each person writes caption on previous drawings before contributing next drawing. Final square: own drawing plus caption.
(e) One piece of paper only, passed around.
(f) Narrative themes, e.g. 'in prison', 'adrift at sea', 'won the Pools', etc.

219. Animal Consequences

Each person draws the head of an animal, folds paper and passes on. Next person draws body, next one legs. Then each person takes one they have not worked on and talks about it in first person.

Variation: The more conventional one, using people. Each person draws a hat, folds paper, passes on; then face, body, legs, feet, etc.

220. Conversations in Paint (based on No. 155(i))

Start with pairs opposite each other along long sheet of paper. One colour each, start conversation with opposite person (different colour), then let conversations develop with neighbours on either side, etc.

221. Situation Diagrams

Everyone draws a sketch or diagram to represent what they think is (or was) going on in a particular situation in which the group was involved. Discuss everyone's diagrams in the group, perhaps classify them. This is described in more detail in *Illuminative Incident Analysis* by D. Cortazzi

and S. Roote (McGraw Hill, New York, 1975).
Variation: To plan action, draw diagram of situation and consider silently (two minutes) possible actions, then discuss.

222. Sociograms

The group draws diagrams to illustrate graphically community relationships, or relationships between individuals.
Variations:
(a) Use 3-D materials such as polystyrene balls, wire, string and paint.
(b) Can be used to present graphically information about the group, e.g. answers to the question 'Who in the group do you know best?'
(c) Can be used to plot number of verbal communications from each person to each other person, to give an 'interaction picture'.

223. Brainstorming Flow Diagram

The group starts with a key word in the middle of the paper, e.g. JOB or ANGER, etc. Everyone adds any other words that occur to them in 'thought-streams'. Then any word that has cropped up can be taken as a basis for individual painting.

224. Visual Whispers

First person shows second a drawing, then asks him/her to sketch it from memory. Second person shows this to third person, who in turn sketches it from memory. Compare last drawing with first. Discuss the sort of distortions which occur.

225. Newspaper Games

These are co-operative games for small groups (4-7) which can then compare results with other groups.
(a) Animal shapes. Each small group has to tear an animal shape out of newspaper, one turn each, no speaking.
(b) Fashion model. Each group makes an outfit for a model from newspapers.
(c) Building a tower. Each group builds a self-standing tower, to be judged by height, stability and originality (jury formed by members from each group). Allow one hour.
(d) As (c), but time-limit of half an hour and repeat three times:
    (i) verbal communication allowed;
    (ii) no verbal communication;
    (iii) single words only.

226. Using Magazine Pictures

Everyone selects a magazine picture they like and these are pinned up.

Group writes down qualities of picture chosen, then associations to each picture are shared in group.

Variations:

(a) Choose pictures disliked.

(b) Given a few photographs from magazine, small groups think up articles to fit them. A 'reporter' tells the story to the large group.

(c) Pairs choose a magazine photograph which shows two people communicating, and perform the conversation they might be having. The group guesses which photograph it is.

227. *Trading Skills*

The group is divided into two halves, and both groups have sheets of paper. One group is given materials, e.g. collage materials, paint, etc. The other group is given equipment — scissors, glue, brushes, etc. The two groups have to 'trade' with each other to provide a collage/painting, etc. People can work individually, in small groups, or as a whole group. The theme can be chosen to reflect conflict at some level (interpersonal, community, national, international) or left to the group. There are many possibilities in trading, e.g. fair trading, 'driving a hard bargain', etc. The discussion will include what took place, and particular sources of conflict, together with any solutions discovered.

228. *Art Arena Games*

These are co-operative team games developed by Don Pavey and his colleagues, and described fully in *Art-Based Games* by Don Pavey (Methuen, London, 1979). The aim is to create a mural from the contributions of two groups (two to four members in each). Below is a summary of the stages involved in an adapted version by Suzanne Charlton (see 'Art Therapy with Long-Stay Residents of Psychiatric Hospitals' in *Art as Therapy*, edited by Tessa Dalley (Tavistock, London/Methuen, New York, 1984)):

(a) Fix a large sheet of paper to a wall for the mural.

(b) Divide into two equal groups.

(c) Choose a theme (e.g. a pattern, sunshine and storm, birds, space exploration, carnival) in which two contrasting ideas have to be combined.

(d) Each group chooses colours and shapes to represent their group.

(e) Members of each group draw and paint their own images on separate sheets of paper and cut them out.

(f) Both groups, working at separate tables, arrange layouts for their designs.

(g) The mural. Two people (one member from each group) take turns to transfer a cut-out shape on to the mural until all the shapes have been used.

(h) Everyone makes suggestions on moving shapes around to improve the final result.
(i) Discussion of result and process. Some relevant questions might be:
Is the result a unified picture or not?
Was the game enjoyable or stressful?
Did people co-operate, or were there problems?

K *Guided Imagery, Dreams and Meditations*

This section includes techniques which aim to get in touch with parts of our consciousness of which we are normally unaware. Some of the images arising from these techniques can be quite powerful, and it is important to ensure that people can return to 'normal life' at the end of their experience. The section falls into three parts:

Guided Imagery
Dreams, Myths and Fairy Tales
Painting as Meditation

GUIDED IMAGERY

Preparation for Visualisations

Before listing some of the themes, let us look at the method itself and the preparation needed to approach it. These themes are often also called 'guided fantasies', but as they often include a mixture of fantasy and reality, the concepts of 'imaginative journeys' and 'visualisations' seem more accurate.

The basic method is as follows, in its barest outline. Starting with some relaxation exercises, the leader of the group tells a story, or describes a scene, concentrating on the sort of details that bring back memories or evoke feelings. After returning from the 'trip', everyone paints an image from it (or, if it is preferred, everyone shares experiences verbally). There are several important points to be borne in mind if you are thinking of using imaginative journeys or visualisations with a group, and I have listed these, together with some examples of what can go wrong:

(a) Suitability. They are not appropriate for very disturbed people, and work best with groups that can concentrate enough to listen well. Even if there is only one person who is too disturbed, or who cannot concentrate, this may be enough to spoil the experience for others. People also need to be able to relax in order to 'get into' imaginative journeys, so if this is a

major problem, this method is not suitable for that group.

The main point of many of these journeys and visualisations is to tap unacknowledged parts of the person, and become aware of them, such as hidden needs, or strengths. The extent to which this is possible depends on the insight of the people concerned. For people with little insight, the journeys will remain at their face value, but can nevertheless be worthwhile.

(b) Different Levels of Experience. They can be used on several different levels; for instance, as story-telling with children or mentally handicapped people, to stimulate their imagination; or as an approach to any theme for adults, to help them feel their way into it. At a deeper level, they can bring up some very powerful images, which can stay with people and sometimes be very upsetting. So care is needed to keep the level light enough for people to cope; if this is done, they can lead to enjoyable and worthwhile experiences.

Example 1: A group of children were asked to imagine themselves going for a walk in the sunshine, along a path that led into a green field. What was in the field? This led to an enjoyable session with many imaginative paintings.

Example 2: A group of professionals were asked to make an imaginative journey to a place they knew and which had special memories, and then do a painting. It was intended to be a positive experience, but the 'special memories' for one person included some acute pain in the resulting painting. This produced a total catharsis which was inappropriate in that particular setting, unexpected for the therapist, and destructive because it was unresolved.

(c) Levels of Relaxation. Some means of relaxation are needed at the beginning, and the level chosen may influence the depth of the subsequent experience. At the lightest level, members of the group just close their eyes so that they can 'see' the images in the story as the leader tells it. A useful mid-level of relaxation can be reached by asking people to sit in easy-chairs, or back to back on the floor, and going through some simple relaxation exercises (close eyes, let go of bags, open hands, feel chair/floor, feet on ground, comfortable ...). A deeper relaxation is achieved with the group lying on the floor (eyes closed) and people are in a state of greater suggestibility in this state; this can be too much for some groups, and can be inappropriate in some settings (e.g. short-term groups in which little is known about the participants).

(d) The Journey or Visualisation. When people are relaxed, the leader tells a story consisting mainly of images, concentrating on the sort of details that enable people to bring back memories, or to visualise their own version of what is being described. It is important to tell the story or describe the

journey slowly to allow people time to select the right memory or see their own details, e.g. of a tree; this process is important and cannot be hurried. Practice is needed to find out what the right pace is.

Example 3: In one group, the leader hurried through the instructions too fast, and the group prepared to do paintings without their usual enthusiasm. It turned out that they all felt that they had been whisked through the journey so fast that they had not stayed with any images long enough to be able to paint them. So the leader had to start again and go through it more slowly. This time everyone had a personal image to paint and found the session interesting and rewarding.

(e) Coming Back. Often in imaginative journeys there is a definite transition point to 'another world', e.g. a door in a garden wall. It is most important to bring people back through that door, and back into present time.

Example 4: A group of psychiatric patients were taken on an imaginative journey to outer space, where they landed on a planet and painted, danced or dramatised what it was like. However, they were never brought back, and the group remained disturbed — not only for the rest of the day, but for several weeks in relation to the sessions.

(f) Painting. At the end of the trip, everyone is asked to paint an image of their trip, and this is usually a period of quiet concentration in which people are still 'digesting' their experience. Verbal sharing is probably most usefully left until after this unless there is an obvious need for it.

(g) Support. It is important to allow time to talk at the end, and to have adequate support available, in case this is needed. Even well-planned sessions can be unpredictable.

(h) Further Reading. There is a whole chapter on Fantasy Journeys in *Awareness* by John Stevens (Bantam Books, New York, 1973), including further instructions for leaders, emphasising how each person's experience must be respected. See also *Mind Games* by R. Masters and J. Houston (Turnstone Books, London, 1973) and more recently *Guided Affective Imagery* by Hanscarl Leuner (Thieme-Stratton, New York, 1984); and for background history, *Seeing with the Mind's Eye: The History, Techniques and Uses of Visualisation* by Mike and Nancy Samuels (Random House, New York, 1975). Also *Guide to Stress Reduction* by L. John Mason (Peace Press, Culver City, California, 1980).

To conclude, here is a first-person account of a visualisation which resulted in a positive experience:

After a session of movement exercises and a short meditation, we all lay down on the floor and relaxed. Sarah read the 'Wiseperson' visualisation from a book, very slowly and deliberately with long pauses [see No. 230]. I was in a forest in springtime, with newly clad beech trees all round. When I approached the fire, the person I met was my favourite adopted aunt, who died several years ago. I asked her whether I was making the right decision (I was considering leaving my job to go on a course). She beamed at me and said: 'You always make wonderful decisions!' She picked up a single new leaf on a twig from the ground, and gave it to me. At first, I was disappointed with my gift and thought: 'Is that all?', but later I realised the freshness of the leaf represented enjoyment of the present moment, which was something I could have at any time and was worth more than any more durable object. Later, I did a painting of myself, my adopted aunt, the fire and the leaf, with a huge beech tree framing them. Doing this painting helped me to absorb the experience, which I found very encouraging.

Imaginative Journeys

Below are a few examples of imaginative journeys. In each case, you remain yourself in the journey. Only the 'bare bones' are given, and details need to be filled in to make each one seem more 'real'; this can be done by thinking through the journey beforehand.

229. Magic Carpet Ride

Outdoors on a beautiful spring day ... sunshine ... imagine being on a magic carpet, free to travel anywhere without any effort ... feel yourself floating off the ground ... go as high as you wish ... look down ... remain calm and relaxed ... go anywhere you want ... take a few minutes for your journey ... return ... savour any special moment.

230. Wiseperson Guide

Outdoors on a calm sunny day ... find self in clearing in wood ... notice smells and sounds ... feels very safe ... path leads up through woods ... come to a clearing ... fire in middle ... on other side of fire is your wiseperson guide, waiting quietly ... place log on fire ... go and sit with wiseperson ... what is she/he like? ... when ready, ask a question ... listen for answer ... rest a while, and thank your guide ... she/he embraces you as you leave and gives you a gift in memory of your meeting ... back down the path calmly ... to first clearing.

231. Gifts

You are in a beauty spot by a warm lagoon ... you dive in, find some underwater rocks ... there is a cave ... you swim through ... find an opening

... then meet someone who gives you a gift ... you receive this and return through the cave. Afterwards, paint the person you met and the gift you received.

232. Secret Garden and House

You are walking through some woods ... find a path ... follow it ... come to a gate in a wall ... go through ... private/secret garden ... explore it ... see a house ... decide whether to go in or not ... what is it like? ... maybe meet someone ... what happens? ... and return through gate and path.

233. Secret Cave

Go for a walk ... come to a meadow ... sunshine ... tree ... flowers ... look at them, feel and smell them ... stream ... boat ... into a tunnel ... secret cave ... what do you find? ... returning from the cave ... and so back home.

234. Doorway

Go for a walk ... find a doorway ... what is it like? Familiar or unfamiliar? ... decide to open the door ... is it hard or easy? ... open the door and go through ... what do you find?

235. Mountain View

Pastoral scene ... mountains ... climb up ... describe the journey ... reach the top ... look at the view ... meet special person ... what sort of conversation do you have? ... ask that person a question ... what do you ask? ... what is the reply? ... come down from the mountain.

236. Magic Shop

Going out for a trip ... visit a sleepy old village ... find a shop ... a magic shop ... what do you find in it? ... what do you take back with you? (Or a magic junk-shop in a backstreet of a busy town ...)

237. Boat Journey

Starting out in a boat ... where does it start from? ... where is it going? ... what is the journey like? ... how does it end? Make up your own story, and then draw or paint it.

238. Shipwrecked on an Island

You are shipwrecked on an island ... you land ... what is it like? ... what do you do first? ... if you are part of a group, what do you decide to do all together? ... how do you get rescued? ... what do you feel when you return?

239. Five Senses

Use imagery which appeals to all five senses, since many people have a greater sensitivity to some senses than to others, e.g. setting sail in boat: see ripples, smell and taste salt tang, feel wind, hear waves slapping against boat, etc.; then land on island and see what it is like.

Identifications

These are visualisations in which you 'become' something or somebody else, and identify with the feelings you imagine they might have.

240. Rosebush

Imagine you are a rosebush ... where are you growing? ... how big? ... what sort of roses? ... feel your roots ... and your branches ... what is your life like? ... how does it change with the seasons? ... what do you feel about it? Afterwards, paint your rosebush, and talk about it in the first person, as it was in the visualisation.

241. Natural Objects

Visualisations of self as tree, flower, house, etc. A flower is a good one to start with, as for most people this is an image without negative meanings.

242. Dialogues

Dialogues between some of these, e.g. visualisations of self as a tree-stump, then a cabin, then a stream, followed by dialogues between any of these.

243. Moving Objects

Visualisations of self as a moving object, such as an animal or motorbike.

244. River

Image of a river — imagine being the source of a stream (source) ... which tumbles down (childhood) ... into a bold and powerful river (youth) ... becomes a larger river, polluted and carrying cargo (responsibility) ... then to an estuary ... and finally the sea (loss of ego).

245. Mythical Character

Imagine being a mythical character ... setting out on a journey ... where to? ... having adventures ... what sort of adventures? ... finally arrive home again. After the journey do a painting about the journey or one aspect of it.

Other Ways of Stimulating Imagery

246. Group Fantasy

Heads in a circle, one person starts with what she/he sees in imagination, then another takes over, creating group fantasy.

247. Listening to Music

Use music to create atmosphere, e.g:
　　Ravel: *Daphnis and Chloe*
　　Brahms: *Symphony No. 1 in C (3rd Movement)*
　　Respighi: *The Pines of Rome*
　　Debussy: *Girl with the Flaxen Hair*
　　Other music with pleasant-feeling possibilities

248. Breathing in Light (can be a good way to end a session)

Breathe deeply ... be aware of the group as a circle ... imagine glow of light round each person ... gradually watch light join into complete circle ... notice how far light spreads out ... follow it gently ... imagine breathing in this light ... going down into chest ... spreading into body ... name each part ... and out through fingers and toes ... feel the light and warmth ... come back to familiar self and open eyes.

DREAMS, MYTHS AND FAIRY TALES

249. Working with Dreams

Paint a dream or nightmare you have had, especially one that is important or recurrent, or most recent.
Variations:
(a) If dreams are not remembered, paint a daydream or fantasy.
(b) Use Gestalt technique (see Part One, Chapter 2, Section 12) on images in dream painting, to explore them in the present tense.
(c) With an unhappy dream, create (visually or verbally) a more satisfactory ending.
(d) Keep a journal of dreams and thoughts arising, in words or pictures.
(e) Write a poem about the dream or painting of it (the abbreviated forms of poetry lend themselves to expressing dream images).

250. Daydreams and Fantasies

Make up a fantasy story in six small pictures. Or specify the kind of story: adventure, day you would like, etc.
Variations:
(a) Close eyes and look inside — paint what you see.
(b) Paint any fantasy or daydream you have.

(c) Deal with people you know in a series of fantasy drawings.
(d) Paint your New Year's resolutions.
(e) Select from various landscape photographs and create a fantasy about your place.

251. Clay Monsters

Create a 3-D monster from fantasy or dreams.

252. Stories and Strip Cartoons

Draw out a page into boxes and make up a story of any kind (useful way to start if timid).
Variations:
(a) Changing a picture into something different in three moves.
(b) Strip cartoons.

253. Myths

Write or paint the story of your life as a myth.
Variations:
(a) Imagine stepping into a parallel world, the Essential Myth of yourself, of which your everyday self is only a small part. Paint your myth.
(b) Draw identifications with personal heroes and villains, and act them in a play.

254. Fairy Tales

Using a traditional fairy tale as a starting point, read aloud. Then everyone does a painting, open-ended or on a specified aspect, and meets to discuss.
Variations:
(a) Ask people to change the ending, or stop before the end and ask people to supply their own ending, or imagine the next scene.
(b) Use any sort of story in the same way.

PAINTING AS MEDITATION

255. Meditative Drawing and Painting

Close eyes, relax and concentrate on bodily sensations. Stay with body awareness until you have clear images, then draw abstractly to communicate experience.
Variations:
(a) Concentrate on a sound, word or syllable.
(b) Meditate or focus on a particular object: an apple, a stone, etc., in its entirety, and make brush marks to express feelings.
(c) (Zen technique) Imagine becoming the essence of the selected object. Draw during or after.

(d) Use clay as reflective medium after an intense experience.

(e) Make clay pinch-pot, and stay centred so pot becomes balanced.

256. Mandala Possibilities

A mandala is a balanced, centred design, in which opposites are integrated. Mandalas are found in illustrations of Eastern mythology, and Jung paid great attention to them. It is often a good idea to start a session on mandalas with some sort of relaxation or meditation, to become aware of a centre for the mandala, and of the opposites to work with. Some ideas for mandala possibilities:

(a) Your day and your night, and the transitions from one to the other.

(b) The present year, or your lifespan.

(c) Your body, top and bottom, right and left, front and back.

(d) Inner and outer experience; thinking and feeling; masculine and feminine.

(e) Make a mandala with another person, exploring differences and relationships.

(f) Mandala of balanced colours.

(g) Mandalas using stories of gardens, e.g. Garden of Eden, Story of Buddha, etc. (see C. Jung, *Man and His Symbols* (Aldus/Jupiter, London, 1964).

257. Autogenic Training

This is a progressive relaxation technique which can be done using art therapy methods as well as the more conventional verbal methods. It is useful for dealing with chronic problems, physical and mental.

(a) Relaxation Exercise. After body relaxation, paint with watercolour brush in leisurely way, broad horizontal bands of colour with varying tones of greens, blues and purples, being aware of paint spreading across the page. Continue until in relaxed state.

(b) Visualisation. With eyes closed, visualise a pleasant experience, and verbalise it. Then paint your visualisation.

(c) Make another painting, or clay model of how you felt during your trip.

(d) Paint or sculpt your problem, and compare with any work on this theme before the relaxation.

For further details, see Chapter 22 in *Clinical Art Therapy* by Helen Landgarten (Brunner/Mazel, New York, 1981) and *Guide to Stress Reduction* by L. John Mason (Peace Press, Culver City, California, 1980).

258. Colour Meditations

These are done on wet paper using water colour paints and soft brushes. Thoroughly wet the paper (cartridge or water colour paper) and smooth down on to flat board (plywood is good), easing out air bubbles from the centre with a sponge. Then apply one particular colour and watch what happens. The process of doing colour washes can be treated as a relaxation or meditation. Combinations of different colours can evoke different feelings and give rise to definite forms which 'grow' out of the painting. This is the method developed by members of the Anthroposophical Movement based on the work of Rudolf Steiner. For further details, consult one of the following:

The Mystery Wisdom of Colour — Its Creative and Healing Powers, by Gladys Mayer.

Colours: A New Approach to Painting by Gladys Mayer.

The Individuality of Colour by Elisabeth Koch and Gerard Wagner.

The Creative Power of Colour by Hilde Boos-Hamburger.

All from the Rudolf Steiner Press, 38 Museum Street, London WC1A 1LP.

L Links with Other Expressive Arts

Art is often used in conjunction with movement, drama, poetry and music. The ideas in this section are ones which specifically combine art with another mode of expression. There is an infinite number of ways of combining different expressive arts, and those given below are only a few of the possibilities. Those wanting to develop this area should consult the book list at the end of this book for ideas in other expressive arts such as drama and music. This section looks at art combined with the following other expressive arts:

Movement
Drama
Poetry
Sound and Music
Multi-media

Movement

259. Trust Walks

In pairs, lead each other on a blind walk, introducing partner to as many textures as possible. Come back and paint the experience.
Variations:
(a) Paint the experience of being the leader or of being led.
(b) Paint as a group on a large sheet of paper.
(c) Do breathing exercises, then draw how you feel afterwards.
(d) Touch hands and faces of others (eyes closed), remember any images passing through mind; write or draw these afterwards.

260. Emotions

Use movement to explore and express emotions, then paint the experience, e.g:
(a) Meeting as friends and as enemies.

(b) The sea: group in circle expresses moods of ocean waves, calm, storm, etc.

(c) Move to music.

261. Gesture Drawings

Make marks on paper with a gesture communicating an inner feeling. These can be developed into a larger picture.

Variations:

(a) Make marks on separate pieces of paper and play a guessing game with others as to which was which.

(b) Choose pairs of opposites, e.g. anger and calm, joy and despair, etc.

(c) Try with left and right hands.

(d) Imagine hand is a bird swooping, ant crawling, bulldozer, etc., and change colour each time. Move to new sheet of paper when full. Choose ways you like best and least, and contemplate differences.

(e) See also No. 195(b) — movements of different qualities.

(f) Make vigorous movements to describe stance and rhythm of an object, and repeat them until you can 'feel' the object. Then record these feelings on a large piece of paper.

(g) Close eyes, draw pattern in the air with hand, and develop into a rhythm. Then transfer it to paper and give it a title.

(h) As in (g), but start by imagining a good feeling.

262. Acting Sensations

Imagine moving through peanut butter, or syrup, etc. Act it and then paint the sensation.

263. Dance

After dancing as a group, paint feelings on large piece of paper.

Drama

264. Sculpting Situations

Each person draws a diagram of how she/he feels about the group, preferably abstract. Each person's diagram is then used to create a human sculpture from the group. The person who did the drawing alters the sculpture if not correct.

Variations:

(a) Let the sculptures 'come alive' and see what happens.

(b) Make models from clay or plasticine, then act situations using the models. This can be done at many levels.

(c) See also Family sculptures — Nos. 129 and 148.

(d) See also No. 193 — Group roles, and No. 194 — Role-playing.

265. Dialogues

Use contrasts or conflicts which arise from a painting or model to develop a dialogue, e.g. between a hard and soft aspect of self. Invent voices for each part. After a dialogue, try to see if there is a 'middle way' combining both qualities.

266. Action and Conflict Themes

Combine painting and drama around any suitable themes, e.g:
(a) No. 78 — Action and conflict themes.
(b) No. 221 — Situation diagrams.
(c) No. 227 — Trading skills.
(d) Themes from other sections.

267. Accidents

Act dramas of accidents and injuries, involving the use of plaster of Paris gauze for sculptures, plaster casts, etc. Good for children.
Variations:
(a) Use plasticine models to rehearse impending difficult situations, operations, hospital stays, etc.
(b) Re-enact any situations which have recently caused distress.
(c) Role reversal, in which children have control. e.g. giving injections, etc.

268. Pictures Come to Life

Everyone draws a picture on a theme connected with their present situation. Then they make their pictures come alive and enact the situation.
Variations:
(a) Develop drama to include any changes people want to make in themselves or their situation.
(b) Pictures of the future, and enact these.

269. Masks

(a) Make masks and use them in improvisations and plays. See also Nos. 86, 165 and 201.
(b) Monster masks: make 'scary monster' masks and use them to act plays and situations. (This can be a useful way of approaching situations involving anger, especially for younger groups.) Sometimes a useful counterpart to this is also to make 'happy monster' masks.

270. Hats

Each person makes a different hat and wears it. Then the group works out a drama to include the different personalities represented.

271. Drama Games

Almost any drama game or 'warm up' can be followed by painting. This gives a chance for reflecting on an experience, although it is not always possible to 'translate' directly from one mode to another. For drama games see the Bibliography at the end of this book.

272. Puppet Theatre

Make puppets and use them in improvisations and plays. There are many kinds of puppets, e.g. glove and finger puppets, string puppets, shadow puppets, full-size puppets; and a variety of materials can be used, e.g. cloth, papier-mâché (see No. 38), junk materials, paper bags, etc.

273. Theatrical Costumes

Draw yourself in theatrical costume (everyday and fantasy). Develop the role and use it in a group inprovisation.

274. Story-telling and Plays

A variety of other activities can be used to stimulate story-telling and play-acting:
(a) Sand play (see No. 36).
(b) Paper figures (see Nos. 26(e) or 135(b)).
(c) Imaginary traffic system (see No. 52).
(d) Add images to a group painting, telling the story as it proceeds (see No. 182).
(e) Masks (see Nos. 86, 165, 201 and 269).
(f) Puppets (see No. 272).
(g) Some other themes from previous sections which lend themselves to dialogues and plays:
   D: No. 46
   F: Nos. 84, 99, 104, 109
   G: Nos. 127, 129, 133, 145, 148
   H: No. 170
   I: Nos. 185, 188
   J: Nos. 226, 227
   K: Nos. 249, 253

275. Tape Recorder

Use a tape recorder to describe paintings afterwards, or make associations with particular images (some people find tape recorders very inhibiting, others find them very liberating).
Variations: In pairs, interview each other about artwork done.

Poetry

276. *Poetry as Stimulus*

Use poetry read aloud as a stimulus for painting. Evocative poetry open to many interpretations works best, e.g. *Ode to Autumn* (Keats), *The Prophet* (Khalil Gibran), nonsense poems such as *Jabberwocky* (Lewis Carroll) etc.
Variations:
(a) Poetry reading as an activity in its own right.
(b) Responding to poetry with more poetry.

277. *Poetry as Response*

As a change from painting, individuals can respond in poetry or word form to a group experience. This is particularly useful when the group has produced a painting telling a group story (see No. 181).

278. *Concrete Poetry*

This gives visual shape to words, and combines words into an image, e.g. a poem about a fish in the shape of a fish; words placed in such a way as to express their meaning.

Sound and Music

279. *Sounds into Paint*

Sit in a circle and make the same sound for 30 seconds, all together. Then walk about briskly, making all sorts of odd sounds. Next, stand back to back in the centre and make a silly sound. Finally, go to your own place at the edge of the room, put your hands over your ears and listen for your own inner sound. Start making it, continuing as you take your hands off your ears and become aware of others. Total time for this is about two minutes. Then do a painting of whatever occurs.
Variation: With eyes closed, make a sound and draw to it for 10 minutes, then open eyes and elaborate design.

280. *Name Sounds*

Dramatically enunciate own name, with body movement to match. Identify other members by sound and gesture, and draw these.

281. *Moulding Sounds*

Use clay to mould into shapes appropriate to particular sounds, preferably with eyes closed.

282. Painting to Music

Paint to music in any way that it moves you. This can be done as an individual or as a group. Music which has a range of moods and is not too well known is most suitable. Some suggestions:

Classical

Bach; Beethoven symphonies; Berlioz: *Symphonie Fantastique*; Dvorak: *Piano Concerto*; Mahler symphonies; Vivaldi: *Concerto for Two Guitars*

Modern

Beatles; jazz; Mike Oldfield: *Ommadawn*; Ravi Shankar; Tibetan bells

Variations:

(a) Listen to the music first, then play again and paint to it.
(b) Listen to the music several times, and paint images evoked afterwards.
(c) Paint to the music quickly, using a succession of sheets of paper.
(d) Compare reactions to music, preferences, feelings evoked, images, etc.
(e) Some good music for children: *Peter and the Wolf, Swan Lake*, etc.
(f) See also No. 195.

Multi-media

283. Letters (for children)

Make letters of the alphabet using dancing, music and painting.

284. Evocative Adjectives

Choose an evocative adjective, and express it in several different modes, e.g. percussion, words, movement, paint.

285. Stimulus to Paint

Use any medium — music, poetry, short story, movement, dance, etc. — to stimulate feelings which can be painted.

286. Response to Paint

Respond to paintings in terms of poetry, song, movement, etc.

287. Sensory Awareness

This exercise aims to improve awareness of the environment and draw attention to sensory experience. (This is 'Denner's Technique', which is based on the theory that emotional tensions block perception.) Objects are provided to look at, smell, listen to and touch. Then rhythms, curves and other impressions are transferred to huge sheets of paper on the wall or floor and are continued into a free-flowing drawing.

Variations:

(a) Lie down, eyes closed, explore world around using smell, touch, hearing. Then move about, contacting objects and people. Open eyes and draw picture of world experienced.

(b) Use all five sense to examine objects, colours, shapes, sounds, and see what feelings are evoked. Find an appropriate means of expression for these.

288. Music and Movement

Move to music in the way it suggests, or according to a particular theme (see *Awareness* by John Stevens (Bantam Books, New York, 1973)). Then paint this experience. Some themes and suitable music:

(a) Compression and expression: Erik Satie's piano music.

(b) Cocoon: Debussy's *Reverie.*

(c) Gravity: Tchaikovsky's *Dance of the Sugar Plum Fairy.*

(d) Exploring possibilities: African drumming.

(e) Dancer: Borodin's *In the Steppes of Central Asia.*

(f) Growing: Erik Satie's or Chopin's piano music.

(g) Evolution: Gabr Szabo's piano music.

(h) Separation and connection: Aaron Copland's *Clarinet Concerto.*

289. Series of Sessions

Plan or evolve a series of sessions involving use of different media, as seems appropriate, e.g. movement to music, mural painting, drama, dance, poetry, relaxation, etc. This can be structured around a common theme or evolve from week to week.

290. Multi-media Events

Plan events and sessions round a theme (e.g. Solidarity — No. 185), using painting, music, poetry, drama, etc.

M *Media Cross-reference*

This part simply indicates by number themes, games and exercises which mention particular media. Many others can, of course, be adapted for use with a desired medium.

1. *Pencils* ⎫
2. *Crayons* ⎬ almost all the ideas in this book
3. *Paint* ⎭
4. *Collage:*
   - C. Media Exploration: Nos. 9, 10, 27, 28, 32, 34
   - D. Concentration, Dexterity and Memory: Nos. 43, 45, 53, 54, 55, 56, 58, 61, 62, 65
   - F. Self-perceptions: Nos. 80, 82, 83, 84, 91, 93, 94, 95, 99, 106, 113, 116, 117
   - G. Family Relationships: Nos. 127, 146
   - H. Working in Pairs: Nos. 157, 163, 165, 169
   - I. Group Paintings: Nos. 186, 187, 188, 189, 192
   - J. Group Games: Nos. 226, 228
   - K. Guided Imagery, Dreams and Meditations: No. 250
5. *Clay:*
   - C. Media Exploration: Nos. 35, 37, 39
   - F. Self-perceptions: Nos. 81, 82, 85, 103, 104, 106, 113
   - G. Family Relationships: Nos. 127, 129, 135, 148
   - H. Working in Pairs: Nos. 167, 169
   - I. Group Paintings: Nos. 183, 186, 191, 193
   - J. Group Games: No. 197
   - K. Guided Imagery, Dreams and Meditations: Nos. 251, 255, 257
   - L. Links with Other Expressive Arts: Nos. 264, 281
6. *Other 3-D and Junk Materials:*
   - C. Media Exploration: Nos. 10, 21, 26, 27, 31, 32, 33, 34, 36, 37, 38, 40, 41
   - D. Concentration, Dexterity and Memory: Nos. 46, 52, 66, 69
   - F. Self-perceptions: Nos. 81, 82, 83, 85, 103, 109
   - G. Family Relationships: Nos. 129, 132, 135, 148, 149, 150

199

H. Working in Pairs: No. 169
I. Group Paintings: Nos. 186, 189, 191, 193
J. Group Games: Nos. 202, 222, 225, 227
L. Links with Other Expressive Arts: Nos. 264, 266, 267, 270, 272, 274

7. *Masks:*

C. Media Exploration: No. 38
F. Self-perceptions: Nos. 82, 86, 101, 102, 103, 106, 123, 124
H. Working in Pairs: Nos. 165, 166
J. Group Games: Nos. 201, 206
L. Links with Other Expressive Arts: Nos. 269, 274

N *Media Notes*

This short section includes a few very brief notes on different readily available media and their particular advantages. Only the most usual media are included here.

1. Dry Media

Pencils, crayons, felt-tip markers, etc. These are easier to control than wet or fluid media. This can be important for those with handicaps which make the mechanics of using fluid media difficult. They can also be useful for people starting off, if they are afraid to use paints and need to retain control over their medium to feel safe. On a practical level, many situations allow only dry media, e.g. home visits with materials, rooms which have to be kept clean or have no access to water, sessions which are too short to allow time to set out or clear up, and so on.

Pencils

The easiest to control, but difficult to get a strong effect or blocks of colour. Good-quality ones can be expensive.

Fibre/Felt-tip Pens and Markers

Easy to use, good clear colours. Strong effects possible, but expanses of colour difficult. Good-quality ones can be expensive. Possible to get large easy-to-grip markers.

Wax Crayons

Moderately easy to control, do not wear down quickly, cheap, large sizes available. Sometimes difficult to get good depth of colour. Good for children. Some adults find them difficult because of the associations with childhood.

Oil Pastels

Moderately easy to control, strong colours, variety of textures and blocks of colour possible. Reasonably priced.

Chalks and Pastels

Moderately easy to use, but effects can smudge easily and need fixing. Chalks are cheap, but difficult to get a great range of colours. Artists' pastels contain toxic pigments.

Charcoal

Quite difficult to use, smudges easily, but very good for strong effects and large drawings.

Graphite Sticks

Same purpose as charcoal, but not as smudgy or breakable.

2. Paints

Paints are much more fluid and therefore more difficult to control than dry media, but also much more rewarding in the effects that can be obtained, and more enjoyable to use for many people. The paints below are all used with water.

Water Colours

The most fluid and difficult to control, mistakes cannot be corrected. This can be daunting, but can also help people to accept their mistakes and live with them. Expensive.

Powder Paint

Cheap, but difficult to achieve the desired consistency, and can be messy to use unless pre-mixed. Not very easy to use thickly or to correct mistakes.

Ready-mixed Powder Paint

Thick, easy to use, reasonably cheap. Available in pint plastic bottles. Can achieve strong effects. Changes tone as it dries.

Acrylic and Polymer Paints

Easy to use, variety of textures possible. Paints dry very quickly, mistakes are easy to correct. Can achieve strong effects. Expensive. When dry, not soluble in water, so care needed with brushes.

Fingerpaints

Thick, good tactile quality, good for regression work, and for children. Expensive.

N.B.: Many artists' quality paints are toxic, so use scholastic materials.

3. Brushes

It is important to have a good range of sizes, especially larger ones.
Hog, Bristle, Nylon: range of sizes up to size 12, for general use, round and square.
Sable, Ox-hair or Squirrel-hair: a few fine brushes for detailed work.
Decorating Brushes: for large-scale work.
Sponges on Sticks: interesting alternative to brushes.
Adaptations (if needed): use holders, bandages or plastic balls for extra grips.

4. Paper

This can be an expensive item, but it is worth trying to ensure that a range of sizes is available, including large size. A range of colours is good too, but if money is limited, white, grey or buff will suit most purposes. Paper should be thick enough to be enjoyable to use.

Sugar Paper

Reasonably cheap, good for most paints, charcoal and pastels.

Cartridge

Good for water colour paints and drawing. Quite expensive. Available in different weights.

Newsprint

Thin and cheap. Can sometimes obtain ends-of-rolls from newspaper offices or stationery firms. Gives large-size paper.

Lining Paper

Cheap. Comes in rolls from decorating suppliers, so needs cutting to size. Rather narrow. Tears easily.

5. 3-D Materials

Malleable 3-D media are good for themes involving strong feelings, especially anger, because people can use some of the energy associated with the feelings to work the media.

Plasticine and Clayola

Easy to use, not messy, easily portable, fairly cheap. Good for children. Some adults find its associations with childhood difficult. Not easy to use for large-scale work.

Play Dough (see No. 39 for recipe)

Good for children. Cheap, easy to make and use.

Clay

Messy, not easily portable, needs firing in a kiln if work is to be kept. Despite these difficulties, working with clay has many more possibilities than plasticine and is a completely different experience in feel and texture. Also good for letting off steam and large-scale projects. Reasonably cheap.

Nylon-reinforced Clay

Does not need firing, can be painted or varnished when dry, but texture not as good as ordinary clay. Also more expensive. Useful in places where no kiln is available.

Junk Materials

Variety of textures and methods of fixing available, large-scale projects possible. Good for using energy if tools are used, such as saw, hammer and nails.

Mask Materials

Gypsona bandage masks, paper bag masks, or pre-formed blank masks (available cheaply in bulk from Theatre Zoo, Drury Lane, London WC2). Masks can also be made from stiff paper, card or papier-mâché over clay or a blown-up balloon (which is later popped).

Other Materials

Plaster, Polyfilla and other materials (see Section C — Media Exploration).

6. Collage Materials

Choosing images and arranging them can be a less daunting first step than actually making images, as it reduces anxiety about 'artistic performance'. It also has a 'distancing' effect in that the images chosen may, but do not have to, relate to the person who chose them. For instance, it may be easier to choose 'angry pictures' from magazines than to paint a picture of one's own anger. Difficult topics may sometimes be approached indirectly in this way.

Other collage materials, such as fabrics, tissue paper, natural objects, junk materials, etc., can be used in addition to other media, or to explore textures and effects of different materials.

7. Adhesives

Copydex

Rubbery emulsion, good for cloth.

Cow gum

Rubber solution, good for paper. Easy to peel off, so useful for shifting positions.

PVA

Water-based emulsion. When dry, not soluble in water. Good for paper, cloth, wood. Useful for collage and general purposes. Can also mix with powder paint to make plastic paint.

Polycell

Good for paper, papier-mâché, etc. Do not use heavy-duty variety containing fungicide.

Evostick Impact Adhesive

Good for sticking wood and other materials quickly.

O *List of Contributors*

A. Art Therapists who took Part in the Survey in 1979

Cherry Ash	Diana Halliday	Patsy Nowell-Hall
David Bostock	Julie Hart	Sue Parsons
Caroline Case	Roger Hart	Michael Pope
Penny Campbell	Diana Hector	Meg Randall
Suzanne Charlton	Robin Holtom	Brian Richardson
Peter Cole	Pat Hurley	Rita Simon
Paul Curtis	Tom Hutter	Claire Skailes
Michael Donnelly	Sarah Kemp	Roger Stanbridge
Karen Drucker	Marion Kerswell	Jo Sutherland
Michael Edwards	Adèle Lambert	Roy Thornton
Douglas Gill	Marian Liebmann	Toril Valland Lowe
Andy Gilroy	Maggie McKiernan	Roger Vickerman
Helen Greenwood	Gerry McNeilly	Felicity Weir
Julia Gudjonsson	Jan Mallett	Chris Wood

B. Further Contributions in 1985 from:

Sheena Anderson	Jim Dymond	Linnea Lowes
Heather Buddery	Tish Feilden	Vicky Morrison
Paul Curtis	Helen Felton	Tessa Roger-Jones
Michael Donnelly	John Ford	Beryl Tyzack
Karen Drucker	Sue Jennings	

P   *Bibliography and Further Reading*

These lists are not comprehensive, but are compiled from those mentioned as useful by various people. Unfortunately the appearance of a title in the list is no guarantee that it is still in print. Those books and articles used for reference and in compiling this collection of themes, games and exercises are marked with an asterisk(*). The books are listed in the following sections for easy reference:

1. Art and Art Therapy
2. Guided Imagery and Visualisation
3. Drama, Drama Games and Drama Therapy
4. Psychodrama
5. Dance Movement Therapy
6. Music Therapy
7. Combined Expressive Arts
8. Games and Exercises for Groups
9. Groupwork
10. Theory of Play and Games
11. Journals
12. Organisations

1. Art and Art Therapy

(a) Books

Adamson, E., *Art as Healing* (Coventure, London and distributed in the US by Samuel Weisen Inc., York Beach, Maine, 1984).

Alschuler, R.H. and Hattwick, L.W., *Painting and Personality* rev. edn. (University of Chicago Press, Chicago, 1969, originally published 1947).

Atack, S., *Art Activities for the Handicapped* (Souvenir Press, London and distributed in the US by State Mutual Books & Periodical Co., New York, 1980).

Betensky, M., *Self-Discovery Through Self-Expression* (C.C. Thomas, Springfield, Illinois, 1973).

Burns, R.C. and Kaufman, S.H., *Actions, Styles and Symbols in Kinetic Family Drawings: An Interpretive Manual* (Brunner/Mazel, New York, 1970 and Constable, London, 1972).

*Cortazzi, D. and Roote, S., *Illuminative Incident Analysis* (McGraw-Hill, New York, 1975).

*Dalley, T. (ed.), *Art as Therapy: An Introduction to the Use of Art as a Therapeutic Technique* (Tavistock, London/Methuen, New York, 1984).

*Denner, A., *L'Expression Plastique, Pathologie, et Réeducation des Schizophrènes* (Les Editions Sociales Francaises, Paris, 1967).

Di Leo, J.H., *Young Children and Their Drawings* (Brunner/Mazel, New York, 1970 and Constable, London, 1971).

——, *Children's Drawings as Diagnostic Aids* (Brunner/Mazel, New York, 1980).

*Donnelly, M. 'The Origins of Pictorial Narrative and its Potential in Adult Psychiatry' (unpublished Research Diploma thesis, Department of Art Therapy, Gloucester House, Southmead Hospital, Bristol, 1983).

Edwards, B., *Drawing on the Right Side of the Brain* (Fontana/Collins, London, 1982 and J.P. Tarcher Inc., Los Angeles, 1979).

Ehrenzweig, A., *The Hidden Order of Art* (Prentice-Hall, Englewood Cliffs, New Jersey, 1970).

Feldman, E.B., *Becoming Human Through Art* (Prentice-Hall, Englewood Cliffs, New Jersey, 1970).

Franck, F., *The Zen of Seeing* (Wildwood House, London, 1974 and Harvard University Press, Cambridge, Mass.).

Goldsmiths College students, *As We See It: Approaches to Art as Therapy* (available from British Association of Art Therapists, c/o 13C Northwood Rd., London N6.

Goodnow, J., *Children's Drawing* (Fontana/Open Books, London, 1977).

Hammer, E.F., *The Clinical Application of Projective Drawings* (C.C. Thomas, Springfield, Illinois, 1958).

Hanes, K.M. (ed.), *Art Therapy and Group Work: An Annotated Bibliography* (Greenwood Press, Westport, Connecticut, 1982).

*Harris, J. and Joseph, C., *Murals of the Mind* (International Universities Press, New York, 1973).

Jameson, K., *Pre-School and Infant Art* (Studio Vista, London, 1968).

*Jung, C.G., *Man and His Symbols* (Aldus/Jupiter, London, 1964 and Dell Publishing Co. Inc., New York, NY, 1968).

——, *Mandala Symbolism* (Bollingdon Series XX, Princeton University, New Jersey, 1973).

Kellog, R., *Analysing Children's Art* (National Press, Palo Alto, California, 1970).

*Keyes, M.F., *The Inward Journey* (Celestial Arts, Millbrae, California, 1974).

Kramer, E., *Art as Therapy with Children* (Schocken, New York, 1978).

——, *Childhood and Art Therapy* (Schocken, New York, 1981).

*Kwiatkowska, H., *Family Art Therapy* (C.C. Thomas, Springfield, Illinois, 1978).

*Landgarten, H.B., *Clinical Art Therapy* (Brunner/Mazel, New York, 1981).

Levick, M., *They Could Not Talk and So They Drew: Children's Styles of Coping and Thinking* (C.C. Thomas, Springfield, Illinois, 1983).

*Liebmann, M.F., 'A Study of Structured Art Therapy Groups' (unpublished MA thesis, Birmingham Polytechnic, 1979).

Lindsay, Z., *Art and the Handicapped Child* (Studio Vista, London, 1972).

Lindzey, G., *Projective Techniques and Cross Cultural Research* (Appleton Century Crofts, New York, 1961).

*Luthe, W., *Creativity Mobilisation Technique* (Grune and Stratton, New York, 1976).

Lyddiatt, E.M., *Spontaneous Painting and Modelling* (Constable, London, 1971).

Melzi, K., *Art in the Primary School* (Blackwell, Oxford, 1967).

Milner, M., *On Not Being Able to Paint* (Heinemann, London, 1971 and International University Press, New York, NY, 1967).

Naumburg, M., *Dynamically Oriented Art Therapy* (Grune and Stratton, New York, 1966).

——, *An Introduction to Art Therapy* (Teacher College Press, Columbia University, New York, 1973).

*Oaklander, V., *Windows to Our Children* (Real People Press, Moab, Utah, 1978).

*Pavey, D., *Art-Based Games* (Methuen, London, 1979).

Pickford, R.W., *Studies in Psychiatric Art* (C.C. Thomas, Springfield, Illinois, 1967).

Plaskow, D., *Art With Children* (Studio Vista, London, 1968).

Prinzhorn, H., *Artistry of the Mentally Ill* (Springer-Verlag, New York, 1972). Translated from *Bildnerei der Geisteskranken* (Springer, Berlin, 1922).

Read, H., *Education Through Art* (Faber, London, 1969).

*Rhyne, J., *The Gestalt Art Experience* (Magnolia Street Publishers, USA; UK contact: Changes Bookshop, 242 Belsize Road, London NW6).
*Robbins, A. and Sibley, L.B., *Creative Art Therapy* (Brunner/Mazel, New York, 1976).
*Rubin, J.A., *Child Art Therapy* (Van Nostrand Reinhold, New York, 1978).
——, *The Art of Art Therapy* (Brunner/Mazel, New York, 1984).
Selfe, L., *Nadia: A Case of Extraordinary Drawing Ability in an Autistic Child* (Academic Press, London, 1977 and Academic Press Inc., San Diego, California, 1978).
*Steiner Painting Techniques:
  Boos-Hamburger, H., *The Creative Power of Colour* (Michael Press and Krisha Press, New York, NY, 1973).
  Koch, E., and Wagner, G., *The Individuality of Colour* (Rudolf Steiner Press and Steinerbooks, Blauvelt, NY, 1980).
  Mayer, G., *The Mystery Wisdom of Colour — Its Creative and Healing Powers* (Mercury Arts Publications).
  ——, *Colour: A New Approach to Painting* (Mercury Arts Publications).
  (All obtainable from Rudolf Steiner Press, 38 Museum St., London WC1).
Strauss, R., *Understanding Children's Drawings* (Rudolf Steiner Press, London, 1978).
Tilley, P., *Art in the Education of Subnormal Children* (Pitman, London, 1975).
*Ulman, E. and Dachinger, P. (eds.), *Art Therapy in Theory and Practice* (Schocken, New York, 1976).
*Ulman, E., and Levy, C.A. (eds.), *Art Therapy Viewpoints* (Schocken, New York, 1980).
*Wadeson, H., *Art Psychotherapy* (John Wiley, New York and Chichester, 1980).
Warren, B. (ed.), *Using the Creative Arts in Therapy* (Croom Helm, London and Brookline Books, Cambridge, Mass., 1984).
Weismann, D.L., *The Visual Arts as Human Experience* (Prentice-Hall, Englewood Cliffs, New Jersey, 1970).
Williams, G.W. and Wood, M.M., *Developmental Art Therapy* (University Park Press, Baltimore, 1977).

Further Titles to be found in:
Art Therapy Bibliography, 1981 (available from British Association of Art Therapists, c/o 13C Northwood Rd., London N6.)

(b) Articles

*Charlton, S., 'Art Therapy with Long-Stay Residents of Psychiatric Hospitals' in T. Dalley, (ed.), *Art as Therapy* (Tavistock, London/Methuen, New York, 1984).
Crompton, C., Chapter on art therapy in *Respecting Children*, Social Work with Young People (E. Arnold, London, 1980).
*Dalley, T. and Wilby, D., 'A Self-Expression Do-it-Yourself Kit', *Therapy*, May 1979.
*Denny, J., 'Techniques for Individual and Group Art Therapy' in E. Ulman and P. Dachinger (eds.), *Art Therapy in Theory and Practice* (Schocken, New York, 1975).
*Gonick-Barris, S.E., 'Art and Nonverbal Experiences with College Students' in A. Robbins and L.B. Sibley, *Creative Art Therapy* (Brunner/Mazel, New York, 1976).
*Holtom, R., 'Imagination Games', *Inscape*, no. 15, May 1977.
*Laing, J., 'Art Therapy in Prisons' in T. Dalley (ed.), *Art as Therapy* (Tavistock, London, 1984).
*Liebmann, M.F., 'The Many Purposes of Art Therapy', *Inscape*, vol. 5, no. 1 (1981).
*Liebmann, M.F., 'Art Games and Group Structures' in T. Dalley (ed.), *Art as Therapy* (Tavistock, London and Methuen, New York, 1984).
*Miller, B., 'Art Therapy with the Elderly and the Terminally Ill' in T. Dalley (ed.), *Art as Therapy* (Tavistock and Methuen, New York, London, 1984).
*Murphy, J., 'The Use of Art Therapy in the Treatment of Anorexia Nervosa' in T. Dalley (ed.), *Art as Therapy* (Tavistock, London and Methuen, New York, 1984).
*Stott, J. and Males, B., 'Art as Therapy for People who are Mentally Handicapped' in T. Dalley (ed.), *Art as Therapy* (Tavistock, London and Methuen, New York, 1984).

(c)　Videotape

Art Therapy produced by T. Dalley and D. Waller, directed by J. Beacham (Tavistock Videotapes, London, 1984).

2.　Guided Imagery and Visualisation

De Mille, R., *Put Your Mother on the Ceiling*, Children's Imagination Games (Walker and Co., New York, 1967).

Leuner, H., *Guided Affective Imagery* (Thieme-Stratton, New York, 1984).

*Mason, L.J., *Guide to Stress Reduction* (Peace Press, Culver City, California, 1980).

*Masters, R.E.L. and Houston, J., *Mind Games* (Turnstone Books, London and Dell Publishing Co., New York, 1973).

*Samuels, M.D. and Samuels, N., *Seeing with the Mind's Eye: The History, Techniques and Uses of Visualisation* (Random House, New York, 1975).

*Stevens, J.O. *Awareness* (Bantam Books, New York, 1973).

3.　Drama, Drama Games and Drama Therapy

Barker, C., *Theatre Games: A New Approach to Drama Training* (Eyre Methuen, London, 1977 and Drama Book Publishers, New York, 1978).

Astoll-Burt, C.A., *Puppetry for Mentally Handicapped People* (Souvenir Press, London and Brookline Books, Cambridge, Mass., 1981).

Courtney, R., *Play, Drama and Thought: Intellectual Background to Drama and Education* 3rd edn. (Cassell, London, 1974).

Courtney, R. and Schattner, G., *Drama in Therapy* (Drama Book Publishers, New York, 1981), vol. 1: children, vol. 2: adults.

Hodgson, J., *Uses of Drama: Acting as a Social and Educational Force* (Eyre Methuen, London, 1977).

Hodgson, J. and Richards, E., *Improvisation* (Eyre Methuen, London, 1968 and Grove Press, New York, 1979).

Jennings, S., *Remedial Drama* 2nd edn (A & C Black, London and Theatre Arts, New York, 1978).

——, *Creative Drama in Group Work* (Winslow Press, Winslow, Buckingham, 1986).

—— (ed.), *Dramatherapy: Theory and Practice for Teachers and Clinicians* (Croom Helm, London, 1986).

Johnston, K., *Impro: Improvisation and the Theatre* (Eyre Methuen, London, 1981 and Theatre Arts, New York, 1979).

Levete, G., *No Handicap to Dance* (Souvenir Press, London and Brookline Books, Cambridge, Mass., 1982)

McClintock, A., *Drama for Mentally Handicapped Children* (Souvenir Press, London 1984).

Scher, A. and Verrall, C., *Hundred Plus Ideas for Drama* (Heinemann, London and Heinemann Educational Books Inc., Portsmouth, New Hampshire, 1975).

Spolin, V., *Improvisations for the Theatre* (Pitman, London and Northwestern University Press, Evanston, Illinois, 1973).

Tomlinson, R., *Disability, Theatre and Education* (Souvenir Press, London, 1982 and Indiana University Press, Bloomington, Indiana, 1984).

Upton, G., *Physical and Creative Activities for the Mentally Handicapped* (Cambridge University Press, Cambridge and New York, 1979).

*Warren, B., *Drama Games for Mentally Handicapped People* (MENCAP, 123 Golden Lane, London EC1Y ORT, 1981).

Way, B., *Development Through Drama* (Longman, London and Humanities Press International Inc., Atlantic Highlands, New Jersey, 1967).

Wethered, A., *Drama and Movement in Therapy* (Macdonald and Evans, London, 1973).

Further booklists may be obtained from The British Association for Dramatherapists, P.O. Box 98, Kirby Moorside, York YO6 6EX.

4. Psychodrama

Blatner, H.A., *Acting In: Practical Applications of Psychodynamic Methods* (Springer Publishing Co. Inc., New York, 1973).

Moreno, J., *Who Shall Survive?* (Beacon House, Beacon, New York, 1953).

——, *Psychodrama* (Beacon House, Beacon, New York, 1975).

Schutz, W., *Joy* (Penguin, Harmondsworth and Grove Press, New York, 1967).

Starr, A., *Psychodrama: Rehearsal for Living* (Nelson-Hall, Chicago, 1979).

5. Dance Movement Therapy

Bate, R., Weir, M., and Parker, C., *Movement and Growth Programmes for the Elderly and Those who Care for Them.* (Association for Dance Movement Therapy Publications, London, 1983).

Bernstein, P., *Eight Theoretical Approaches in Dance Movement Therapy* (Kendall/Hunt, Dubuque, Iowa, 1979).

Caplow-Lindner, E., *Therapeutic Dance/Movement,* Expressive Activities for Older Adults (Human Sciences Press, London and New York, 1979).

Chace, M., *Marian Chace: Her Papers,* C. Harris (ed.), (American Dance Therapy Association, Columba, Maryland, 1975).

Espenak, L., *Dance Therapy: Theory and Applications* (C.C. Thomas, Springfield, Illinois, 1981).

Harris, J.G., *A Practicum for Dance Therapy* (ADMT Publications, London, 1984).

Hartley, L., *Body-Mind Centering: A Therapeutic Approach to the Body and Movement* (ADMT Publications, London, 1984).

Laban, R., *Modern Educational Dance* (Macdonald and Evans, London, 1975).

Lamb, W. and Watson, E., *Body Code: The Meaning in Movement* (Routledge and Kegan Paul, London, 1979).

Leventhal, M. (ed.), *Movement and Growth: Dance Therapy for the Special Child* (New York University Press, New York, 1980).

Levete, G., *No Handicap to Dance* (Souvenir Press, London, 1982).

North, M., *Personality Assessment Through Movement* (Macdonald and Evans, London, 1972).

Payne West, H., *An Introduction to Dance Movement Therapy* (ADMT Publications, London, 1983).

——, *Stepping In: Dance Movement Therapy for the Disordered and Disturbed Child* (ADMT Publications, London, 1984).

Schoop, T., and Mitchell, P., *Won't You Join the Dance?* A Dancer's Essay into the Treatment of Psychosis (National Press Books, Palo Alto, California, 1974).

Spencer, P. (ed.), *Society and the Dance* (Cambridge University Press, Cambridge, 1985).

Further booklists available from the Association for Dance Movement Therapy (ADMT), 99 South Hill Park, London NW3 2SP.

6. Music Therapy

Alvin, J., *Music for the Handicapped Child* (Oxford University Press, Oxford, 1975 and New York, 1976).

——, *Music Therapy* (Hutchinson, London, 1978 and distributed in the US by State Mutual Book and Periodical Service, New York, 1984).

——, *Music Therapy for the Autistic Child* (Oxford University Press, Oxford, 1978 and New York, 1979).

Disabled Living Foundation, *Music and the Physically Handicapped* (DLF, 380-384 Harrow Rd., London W9 2HU, 1970).

Gaston, E., *Music in Therapy* (Macmillan, London and New York, 1968).

McLaughlin, T., *Music and Communication* (Faber, London, 1970).

Moog, H., *The Musical Experience of the Pre-School Child* (Schott, London and European–American Music, Valley Forge, Pennsylvania, 1976).

Nordoff, P. and Robbins, C., *Therapy in Music for Handicapped Children* (Gollancz, London, 1970).

————, *Music Therapy in Special Education* (Macdonald and Evans, London, 1975 and MMB Music Inc., St Louis, Missouri, 1983).

————, *Creative Music Therapy: Individualised Treatment for the Handicapped Child* (John Day, New York, 1977).

Priestley, M., *Music Therapy in Action* (Constable, London, 1975 and MMB Music Inc., St Louis, Missouri, 1984).

Rudd, E., *Music Therapy and its Relationship to Current Treatment Theories* (Magnamusic-Baton, St Louis, Missouri, 1980).

Streeter, E., *Making Music with the Young Handicapped Child* (Music Therapy Publications, 32 Durand Gardens, London SW9, 1980).

Further booklist available from the Association of Professional Music Therapists (Secretary: Steve Dunachie), St. Lawrence Hospital, Caterham, Surrey.

7. Combined Expressive Arts

Adkins, G., *The Arts and Adult Education* (Advisory Council for Adult and Continuing Education (ACACE), 19b de Montfort St., Leicester LE1 7GE, 1980).

The Arts in Schools (Calouste Gulbenkian Foundation, 98 Portland Place, London W1N 4ET, 1982).

Attenborough Report, *Arts and Disabled People* (Bedford Square Press, London, 1985).

Feder, E. and Feder, B., *The Expressive Arts Therapies: Art, Music and Dance as Psychotherapy* (Prentice-Hall, Englewood Cliffs, New Jersey, 1981).

Jennings, S., (ed.), *Creative Therapy*, 2nd edn. (Kemble Press, Banbury, 1983).

Lord, G. (ed.), *The Arts and Disabilities* (Macdonald, London, 1981 and distributed in the US by State Mutual Book & Periodical Service, New York, 1985).

May, R., *The Courage to Create* (Collins, London and Bantam Books Inc., New York, 1976).

Ross, M., *The Creative Arts* (Heinemann, London and Heinemann Educational Books Inc., Portsmouth, New Hampshire, 1978).

Storr, A., *The Dynamics of Creation* (Pelican, Harmondsworth, 1977 and Atheneum, New York, 1985).

Warin, P., *Through a Looking Glass: Access to the Arts for People with Disabilities and Special Needs* (South West Arts, 23 Southernhay East, Exeter EX1 1QG).

Warren, B., *Using the Creative Arts in Therapy* (Croom Helm, London/Brookline Books, Cambridge, Mass., 1984).

Witkin, R., *The Intelligence of Feeling* (Heinemann, London and Heinemann Educational Books Inc., Portsmouth, New Hampshire, 1973).

8. Games and Exercises for Groups

Brandes, D., *Gamesters' Handbook 2* (Hutchinson, London, 1984).

*Brandes, D. and Phillips, H., *Gamesters' Handbook* (Hutchinson, London, 1979).

Brosnan, B., *Yoga for Handicapped People* (Souvenir Press, London and Brookline Books, Cambridge, Mass., 1982).

*Butler, L. and Allison, L., *Games, Games,* collected for Playspace (Short Course Unit, Polytechnic of Central London, 35 Marylebone Rd., NW1 5LF).

Carkhuff, R., *The Art of Helping V,* Trainer's Guide (Human Resources Development Project, Amherst, Massachusetts, 1983).

Fluegelman, A. (ed.), *The New Games Book,* New Games Foundation (Sidgwick and Jackson, London and Doubleday Co. Inc., New York, 1978).

—— (ed.), *More New Games and Playful Ideas,* New Games Foundation (Doubleday, New York, 1981).

Harmin, M., *How to Get Rid of Emotions that Give You a Pain in the Neck* (Argus, Hemel Hempstead, 1976).

*Höper, C., Kutzleb, U., Stobbe, A. and Weber, B., *Awareness Games* (St. Martin's Press, New York, 1976).

*Jelfs, M., *Manual for Action* (Action Resources Group, c/o 13 Mornington Grove, London E3 4NS, 1982).

Jones, R., *Shared Victory: A Collection of Unusual World Records* (Ron Jones, 1201 Stanyan St., San Francisco, California 94117, 1980).

Judson, S. (ed.), *A Manual on Nonviolence and Children* (Philadelphia Yearly Meeting, 1977; obtainable from Nonviolence and Children Program, Friends Peace Committee, 1515 Cherry St., Philadelphia, Pa. 19102).

Kanfer, F.H. and Goldstein, A.P., *Helping People Change: A Textbook of Methods* (Pergamon Press, Oxford and Elmsford, New York, 1980).

*Lewis, H. and Streitfeld, H., *Growth Games* (Souvenir Press, London, 1970 and Bantam, New York, 1971).

Orlick, T., *The Cooperative Sports and Games Book Challenge Without Competition* (Writers and Readers Publishing Cooperative, London, 1982 and Pantheon Books, New York, 1978).

*Pax Christi, *Winners All: Cooperative Games for All Ages* (PC, Blackfriars Hall, Southampton Rd., London NW5, 1980).

Pfeiffer, J.W. and Jones, J.E., *Handbook of Structured Experiences for Human Relations Training* (5 vols., University Associates Publishers and Consultants, La Jolla, California, 1975). Available from University Associates International Ltd, Challenge House, 45/47 Victoria St., Mansfield, Nottinghamshire, NG18 5SU.

*Priestley, P., McGuire, J., Flegg, D., Hemsley, V. and Welham, D., *Social Skills and Personal Problem Solving* (Tavistock Publications, London, 1978 and Methuen, New York, 1979).

Prutzman, P., Burger, M.L. Bodenhamer, G. and Stern, L., *The Friendly Classroom for a Small Planet* (Avery Publishing Group Inc., Wayne, New Jersey, 1978).

*Remocker, J. and Storch, E., *Action Speaks Louder: Handbook of Non-verbal Group Techniques* (Churchill Livingstone, Edinburgh, 1979 and New York, 1982).

World Studies Project London, *Debate and Decision* (c/o One World Trust, 24 Palace Chambers, Bridge St., London SW1A 2JJ).

9. Groupwork

Bannister, D. and Fransella, F., *Inquiring Man* 3rd edn (Croom Helm, London, 1986 and Krieger Publishing Co., Melbourne, Florida, 1982).

*Brown, A., *Groupwork* (Heinemann, London, 1979 and Gower Publishing Co., Greenfield, Vermont, 1980).

Brown, D. and Pedder, J., *Introduction to Psychotherapy: An Outline to Psychodynamic Principles and Practice* (Tavistock, London, 1980 and Methuen, New York, 1979).

Cox, M., *Coding the Therapeutic Process Emblems of Encounter* (Pergamon Press, Oxford and Elmsford, New York, 1978).

*Culbert, S.A., 'The Interpersonal Process of Self-Disclosure: It Takes Two to See One', *Explorations in Applied Behavioral Science,* no. 3 (Renaissance Editions, New York, 1967).

*Douglas, T., *Groupwork Practice* (Tavistock, London and International Universities Press, New York, 1976).

*——, *Basic Groupwork* (Tavistock, London, 1978).

Ernst, J and Goodman, L., *In Our Own Hands: A Book of Self-Help Therapy* (The Women's Press, London, 1982 and J.P. Tarcher, Los Angeles, California, 1981).

*Family Service Unit, *Groups* (FSU, 1976; from FSU, 207 Old Marylebone Rd., London NW1).

Garvin, C.D., *Contemporary Groupwork* (Prentice-Hall, Englewood Cliffs, New Jersey, 1981).

Harris, T.A., *I'm O.K. — You're O.K.* (Pan Books, London, 1973).

Heap, K., *Process and Action in Work with Groups: The Preconditions for Treatment and Growth* (Pergamon Press, Oxford and Elmsford, New York, 1979).

——, *The Practice of Social Work with Groups* (George Allen and Unwin, London and Winchester, Mass., 1985).

*Houston, G., *The Red Book of Groups: A Systematic Approach* (The Rochester Foundation, 8 Rochester Terrace, London NW1, 1984).

Johnson, D.W. and Johnson, F.P., *Joining Together: Group Theory and Group Skills* (Prentice-Hall, Englewood Cliffs, New Jersey, 1982).

Lindenfield, G. and Adams, R., *Problem-Solving Through Self-Help Groups* (Self-Help Associates, 10 Tivoli Place, Ilkley LS29 8SO, 1984).

Rogers, C.R., *Encounter Groups* (Pelican, Harmondsworth, 1973).

Shaffer, J.B.P. and Galinsky, M.D., *Models of Group Therapy and Sensitivity Training* (Prentice-Hall, Englewood Cliffs, New Jersey, 1974).

Shulman, L., *The Skills of Helping: Individuals and Groups* (F.E. Peacock, Itasca, Illinois, 1984).

*Yalom, I.D., *The Theory and Practice of Group Psychotherapy* (Basic Books, New York, 1975).

10. Theory of Play and Games

Axline, V., *Dibs in Search of Self* (Penguin, Harmondsworth, 1973 and Ballantine Books, New York, 1976).

*Bruner, J.S., Jolly, A. and Sylva, K. (eds.), *Play: Its Role in Development and Evolution* (Penguin, Harmondsworth, 1976).

*Caillois, R., *Man, Play and Games* (Thames and Hudson, London, 1962). Translated from *Les Jeux et les Hommes* (Gallimard, Paris, 1958).

Cass, J.E., *The Significance of Children's Play* (Batsford, London, 1971 and David & Charles, North Pomfret, Vermont, 1977).

Culff, R., *The World of Toys* (Hamlyn, London, 1969).

De Koven, B., *The Well-Played Game* (Anchor Books, New York, 1978).

Erikson, E., *Play and Development* (W.W. Norton, New York, 1972).

*——, *Toys and Reasons* (Marion Boyars, London, 1978).

*Garvey, C., *Play* (Fontana/Open Books, London and Harvard University Press, Cambridge, Mass., 1977).

Hartley, R.E., Frank, L.K. and Goldenson, R.M., *Understanding Children's Play* (Columbia University Press, New York, 1952).

*Huizinga, J., *Homo Ludens: A Study of the Play Element in Culture* (Temple-Smith, London, 1970 — 1st English edn, Routledge and Kegan Paul, 1949 and Beacon Press Inc., Boston, Mass., 1955).

Lowenfeld, M., *Play in Childhood* (John Wiley, New York, 1967).

Millar, S., *The Psychology of Play* (Penguin, Harmondsworth, 1968).

*Nicholson, S., *Interactive Art and Play* (Open University Press, Milton Keynes, 1976).

Opie, I. and P., *Children's Games in Street and Playground* (Clarendon Press, Oxford and Oxford University Press, New York, 1969).

*Piaget, J., *Play, Dreams and Imitation in Childhood* (Routledge and Kegan Paul, London, 1951 and W.W. Norton, New York, 1962).

*Winnicott, D.W., *Playing and Reality* (Pelican, Harmondsworth, 1974 and Methuen, New York, 1982).

Journals

Art Therapy

The American Journal of Art Therapy (published in association with the American Art Therapy Association), 6010 Broad Branch Rd., N.W., Washington DC 20015.

The Arts in Psychotherapy, an international journal, ANKHO International Inc., PO Box 426, Fayetteville, NY 13066.

Inscape, the Journal of the British Association of Art Therapists, obtainable from BAAT, c/o 13C Northwood Rd., London N6.

Spectrum, the art magazine for the physically handicapped, available from Conquest, c/o 3 Beverley Close, East Ewell, Epsom, Surrey.

Dramatherapy

Journal of Dramatherapy, available from the British Association for Dramatherapists, PO Box 98, Kirby Moorside, York YO6 6EX.

Dramatherapy Bulletin, available from Dramatherapy Consultants, 6 Nelson Ave., St Albans, Hertfordshire AL1 5RY.

Dance Movement Therapy

Dance Theatre Journal, available from the Laban Centre for Movement and Dance, 14 Laurie Grove, London SE14 6NW.

New Dance, available from Chisenhale, Dance Space, ArtPlace Trust, 64-84, Chisenhale Road, London E3.

Music Therapy

British Journal for Music Therapy, obtainable from The British Society for Music Therapy (Administrator: Denize Christophers), 69 Avondale Ave., East Barnet, Hertfordshire EN4 8NB. The BSMT also publishes conference papers.

Journal of Music Therapy, published by the National Association of Music Therapists, 1133 Fifteenth St. N.W., Suit 1000, Washington DC 2005.

Arts for the Disabled and Disadvantaged

Positif, available from Interlink, 142 The Strand, London WC2R 1HH.

12. Organisations

Art Therapy

British Association of Art Therapists, c/o 13C Northwood Rd., London N6.

Conquest, the society for art for the physically handicapped, c/o 3 Beverley Close, East Ewell, Epsom, Surrey.

Dramatherapy

British Association for Dramatherapists, PO Box 98, Kirby Moorside, York YO6 6EX.

Dramatherapy Consultants, 6 Nelson Ave., St Albans, Hertfordshire AL1 5RY.

Dance Movement Therapy

The Association for Dance Movement Therapy, 99 South Hill Park, London NW3 2SP.
Laban Centre for Movement and Dance, 14, Laurie Grove, London SE14 6NW.
Sesame, Movement and Drama in Therapy, Christchurch, 27, Blackfriars Road, London SE1 8NY.

Music Therapy

Association of Professional Music Therapists (Secretary: Steve Dunachie), St Lawrence's Hospital, Caterham, Surrey.
British Society for Music Therapy (Administrator: Denize Christophers), 69 Avondale Ave., East Barnet, Hertfordshire EN4 8NB.

Arts for the Disabled and Disadvantaged

Interlink (integration through the arts: an international network of arts opportunities for people of all nationalities and cultures who are disabled or disadvantaged), 142 The Strand, London WC2R 1HH.
Shape (working for greater access to the arts for people with disabilities and those who are severely socially disadvantaged), 1 Thorpe Close, London W10 5XL. Also contact this address for details of similar services throughout the UK.

NAME INDEX

217

SUBJECT INDEX

Italics denote references to themes, games
and exercises in Part Two.